Is That All There Is?

Is that ALL? there is

Balancing
Expectation & Disappointment
in Your Life

Dr. DAVID BRANDT

Impact Publishers®
SAN LUIS OBISPO, CALIFORNIA 93406

Impact Publishers and colophon are registered trademarks of Impact Publishers, Inc.

ATTENTION ORGANIZATIONS AND CORPORATIONS:
This book is available at quantity discounts on bulk purchases for educational, business, or sales promotional use. For further information, please contact Impact Publishers, P.O. Box 910, San Luis Obispo, CA 93406-0910 (Phone: 1-800-246-7228).

Library of Congress Cataloging-in-Publication Data

Brandt, David.
    Is that all there is?   :   balancing expectation and disappointment in
  your life   /   David Brandt.
      p.   cm.
    Includes bibliographical references and index.
    ISBN 1-886230-13-7 (alk. paper)
    1. Disappointment.   2.   Expectation (Psychology)   I. Title.
  BF575.D57B73   1998
  158.1--dc21   98.23198
                                                                CIP

Cover design by Kornreich Design Associates, Inc., San Luis Obispo, California
Printed in the United States of America on acid-free paper
Published by **Impact ✍ Publishers**®
POST OFFICE BOX 910
SAN LUIS OBISPO, CALIFORNIA 93406-0910

Dedication

To Laurie — whose abiding love has emboldened, inspired, and sustained me for thirty years.

Contents

Publisher's Note

This publication is designed to provide accurate and authoritative information in regard to the subject matter covered. It is sold with the understanding that the publisher is not engaged in rendering psychological, medical, or other professional services. If expert assistance or counseling is needed, the services of a competent professional should be sought.

Introduction

This book is about the oldest of human experiences — the loss of dreams, the failure of expectations. All of recorded history and literature speak of this theme. Moses descending from Sinai, tablets in hand, profoundly disappointed and rageful as his people prostrated themselves before the golden calf. Napoleon, standing erect at Waterloo, watching his dreams die before British cannon fire. Madame Curie, on the brink of discovery in her laboratory, struggling against repeated failure to unleash the magical powers of radium.

The course of human events is strewn with the remnants of unfulfilled wishes, of outcomes never attained, seeds bearing no fruit. Disappointment is a universal theme. It encompasses the great and the small. We all hope and dream. Inevitably, we are disappointed. Our lives go on, perhaps a little less brightly.

I used to think that disappointment naturally increased when the economic picture was cloudy and the forecast gloomy. But in two decades of tracking it in the culture, my original analysis seems to be only partially true. It turns out disappointment has a remarkable tenacity and resilience and can exist in even the sunniest weather. A padded 401k and an index account at Schwab are no defense against it. In fact, it's when things are brightest —

when you have everything and still don't feel satisfied — that the question "is that all there is?" is most frequently asked.

Disappointment as a cultural phenomenon exists for another reason. The current rate of change is breathtaking and overwhelming. Social changes do not occur smoothly and incrementally, but in a "punctuated equilibrium." The society putters along with a measure of continuity until powerful social forces shake us out of the doldrums and reverberate into every corner of our daily lives. It happened during the renaissance, the industrial revolution, and it's happening now. Technological advances have changed the way information is used, stored, transmitted, and understood and this has affected our relationship to work, community, privacy, and just about everything else. My wife feels more connected because she "internets" daily with a group of college friends she hasn't seen in thirty years. My daughter does her homework without ever setting foot in her school library. She accesses the same data bases as the *New York Times* from her friendly little computer in the bedroom. And I can move my office to the south seas, effectively avoiding the morning commute, without missing that Sunday call to my mother.

Values are changing too. A majority of Americans believe that it's acceptable for a President to lie about marital indiscretions. Family life has been redefined. Husbands and wives both hold jobs in over 80 percent of intact families and the question is no longer "what's for dinner?" but "who's cooking?" Job security and the single-track career have been relegated to the museum of mildewed business practices. And so on. What's all this got to do with disappointment? Simply this. Change involves loss. We give up the old to make way for the new. When people's expectations fail to keep up with these changes, they feel cheated, possibly confused, definitely disappointed.

Many of my patients over the years have complained about feeling chronically disappointed. Many called it by other names: depression, dysphoria, melancholy. But much of what they report is fundamentally the pain associated with lost wishes and dreams. A patient who labeled himself "depressed" was really disappointed in his level of personal accomplishment. Another, who complained of mental fatigue, was anguished by her favorite child's failure to "get his life together." And so forth.

Every era probably has its own characteristic disappointments, but today we suffer from an unparalleled case of inflated hopes and dreams. We expect medical advances to keep us healthy and well into our eighties. We expect the economy to keep rolling along into the next millennium. We expect new technologies to save the earth's ecosystems and protect us from ourselves. Disappointment flourishes in this kind of "everything's possible" environment.

One purpose of this book is to serve as an initial antidote for those whose hopes exceed psychological reality. However, no promises are made. They would merely encourage the very situation we wish to avoid. Instead, I have in mind a larger purpose: to understand the psychology of disappointment. I want to unwrap the mysteries of this troubling experience, show the variety of human responses to it, and reveal, surprisingly, how each of us can use disappointment for our own gain.

There is no real remedy for transitory experiences of disappointment. They come with the territory. Human beings imagine, aspire, and expect. There is risk in dreaming. Chronic disappointment is another matter, however. Some people are repeatedly disappointed in stereotypic ways. Over and over they seem to suffer without realizing why. For them I have suggested a number of attitudinal and behavioral interventions which can be used to break the cycle of pain associated with failed expectations.

I share it with a word of caution. Repetitive patterns of disappointment are fundamentally related to enduring traits in our personalities.

Interventions can have only limited effect without recognition of the relationship between character and expectation. With this in mind, I have emphasized three styles of disappointment in order to demonstrate how particular elements of the individual's character contribute to the kind and extent of experienced disappointment. You will likely find your own story contained within one or more of these categories.

Disappointment comes at you from many directions. Sometimes it is precipitated by failed dreams, other times by dreams coming true and not living up to their advanced billing. "Be careful of what you dream, you just might get it," goes a popular aphorism these days. And the point is well taken. Satisfaction and personal happiness may elude both the well heeled and the unhealed.

The degree to which disappointment interferes with personal happiness can be diminished by knowledge of the disappointment process, the social forces that influence expectation, and the developmental and personality traits which may encourage it. With this information, disappointment becomes an ally, teaching us hard lessons about the limitations of reality and the need for adaptation and flexibility in a constantly-changing universe. I hope this book will provide such knowledge.

Chapter 1

The Best-Laid Plans

The best laid schemes
O' mice and men gang aft a-gley
An' le'e us nought
But grief an' pain for promis'd joy.
— Robert Burns

You're sitting alone at a party. An attractive man approaches and begins a conversation. He has an appealing manner and you find yourself immediately drawn to his quick wit and irreverence. You're just about to tell him so when he gets up, mumbles an excuse, and leaves the room. You're surprised and feel a sense of loss.

You've started a second career after ten years in a profession you found unfulfilling. Retraining required three years of classwork. After some months on the job you discover that much of what you had expected from your second career was only a fantasy. The new work is no more satisfying than the old. You feel frustrated and confused.

You're working very hard on an important proposal for your boss, spending weekends and evenings to perfect your report. You're proud of your effort and submit the proposal with a sense of accomplishment. Your boss reads it a week after submission and writes a short memo that your work was acceptable. You feel resentful and cheated.

You're in bed with your spouse on vacation. This is the first quiet time you have had alone since you left home, although the days have been romantic and you've enjoyed each other. You make love, but the experience is familiar and dull, as if this were any other night. You feel a sense of desperation.

What do you make of these situations? Do they strike a sympathetic chord? Or are they merely the sort of unfortunate circumstances which happen to other people? Chances are, at least one of these experiences will sound familiar to you. If not, perhaps you are one of a small, fortunate, and privileged minority who has never been let down, never suffered from disappointment.

Disappointment is not the sort of subject we like to initiate at dinner parties. It might be appropriate in the therapist's office or at the Complainers' Ball, but not in general conversation. The word disappointment seems too trivial and minor-league to describe our real difficulties. We're all disappointed at some time or another. To depict ourselves as disappointment sufferers doesn't elicit much sympathy or understanding. "Big deal" is the usual response. It's a little like complaining about ingrown toenails. They hurt, but who cares?

Besides, we rarely think of ourselves as disappointed. We prefer "despondent" or "depressed," feeling states that carry more psychological heft. But disappointed we are. Carrying the burden of unmet expectations on our backs, we are like the hikers whose rucksacks increase in weight as they traverse life's many trails. We'd like to get rid of that backpack, but how?

Few people have examined the patterns of disappointment in their lives. At best, they may have encountered the isolated experience, questioning why they should feel so cheated and dismayed and wondering about the power that disappointment holds over them. Still fewer have considered what disappointment really is. What are the ingredients of this bitter soup, sipped with the plastic as well as the silver spoon? We need to ask this important question if we want to relinquish the burden on our shoulders.

What Is Disappointment? The Thoughts and Feelings

Is disappointment merely dissatisfaction? Is it simply an experience of depression or loss? Disappointment certainly contains elements of each, but it is a distinct phenomenon which has existed since the first porridge tasted like clay or the first fire went out. To put it in the simplest of terms, disappointment is unmet expectation. We expected something to happen; it did not; we are disappointed. It involves loss, of course, but not tangible loss, such as the death of a child or the theft of a valued possession. Disappointment is rather the loss of an anticipated idea.

People react differently to disappointment. Some feel anger, despair, defeat. Others do not allow themselves to feel much of anything but confusion. Generally, the most common initial reaction is a sense of shocked dispossession, as if we had lost something dear to us. It is similar to the winning home run miraculously stolen in the last inning by the glove of the opposition center fielder. We feel the loss of an outcome so strongly expected that we nearly assumed it had already happened. We could almost taste it, and therefore we feel cheated, as if, indeed, our team had already won the game. Having been so blatantly robbed, we are alarmed and disbelieving, and these feelings, in turn, are followed by anger, sadness, often self-pity, a sense of loss, and finally acceptance of the unsatisfactory outcome. The disappointment process is a six-stage cycle that follows a general pattern regardless of the content of the expectation or the intensity of the feeling. (For a more detailed discussion of this cycle, see Chapter Three.) Those who are unable to move through the cycle hold onto their discomfort and loss for prolonged periods. Eventually they become resentful and cynical and their world view is laced with misanthropy and pessimism. They become acutely aware of impossibility and focus on the limitations of existence. They appear to be chronically locked in disappointment.

Expectation: Where It All Begins

No one *wishes* for disappointment. We tolerate it as inevitable because we cannot see a means to eliminate it. Alexander Pope wrote: "Blessed is the man who expects nothing for he shall never be disappointed." Was he suggesting that expectation can be eliminated from the human repertoire, thereby preventing disappointment? Is expectation the real problem? Expectation is simply the anticipation of an outcome, but we know it must be more than this by our crestfallen reaction when the outcome is not achieved. Positive expectation really has a dual nature: the belief that an event will occur and the desire for it to do so. Based on past experience, knowledge of the physical universe, or intuition, we anticipate possibility. We form a subjective evaluation of our prospects. And we believe with some certainty that we are correct. But our prognosis is also influenced by our wish for a specific outcome. We hope an event will happen. We look forward to it, and if it fails to occur, we feel bad. The lost idea we spoke about earlier is, in reality, a lost wish.

Examine the illustrations at the beginning of this chapter. Underlying each expectation you will find a wish. The woman at the party hopes her new acquaintance will stay. Perhaps she wishes to develop a relationship or run away to Acapulco with him; we can only speculate about the exact nature of her hopes. But when he leaves, her expectation is unsatisfied. She has been dispossessed of her wish, and she responds with surprise and a sense of loss. The hard-working employee expects a strong positive reaction to match his effort. He wishes for recognition and approval from his boss. When he receives minimal acknowledgment, he feels slighted.

It is the wish contained within every expectation that gives it life and energy. Without the wish an expectation would simply be a probability, a calculated belief about the future. Functioning in computerlike fashion, the mathematical mind might say, "Taking all factors into account, there is a 15 percent chance that my husband will want to make love this evening. With such a low probability I cannot anticipate this will occur." But because we are human we tend to process the same expectation in this manner: "It would be really nice to make love tonight. I know Fred might not be in the mood, but he'll come around." Thus the plan for the evening has been influenced by both probability and wish. The concession to probability is the consideration that Fred might not be in the mood, but the wish carries the day. "He'll come around." In a situation such as this, when a hoped-for outcome gets the better of a realistic assessment of possibility, disappointment is likely and psychological pain is the result.

Can we then be the blessed man or woman without expectation suggested by Alexander Pope? Unlikely. Eliminating expectation is similar to extinguishing curiosity or fantasy. Neither will go away no matter how we program the cognitive computer. The best we can hope for is a diminution. In Samuel Beckett's wonderfully paradoxical play, *Waiting for Godot*, we see the irrational and indefatigable quality of expectation stripped naked. Estragon and Vladimir are waiting for Godot on a bleak country road. He does not come, but sends a messenger in his stead who announces Godot will arrive the next day. The next day arrives. No Godot. Only a messenger with the same announcement. And so on. Yet Estragon and Vladimir persevere. They wait and wait in the face of accumulated time, hoping for Godot to show up. It is an allegory about life. Estragon remarks: "Nothing happens, nobody comes, nobody goes, it's awful!" Finally, after repeated expectation and disappointment:

> Vladimir: *We'll hang ourselves tomorrow. Unless*
> *Godot comes.*
> Estragon: *And if he comes?*
> Vladimir: *We'll be saved.*

The implication is that only hope can save them. Without their wishes, there is no direction, no meaning, nothing. Godot will never come. His arrival is irrelevant. They, however, will continue to expect it.

> Estragon: *I can't go on like this.*
> Vladimir: *That's what you think.*

And their life will be given direction by their expectation:

> Vladimir: *What are we doing here, that is the question.*
> *And we are blessed in this, that we happen*
> *to have the answers.... Yes, in this immense*
> *confusion one thing alone is clear. We are*
> *waiting for Godot to come.*

Is Beckett writing about the absurdity or the necessity of expectation and wish? The matter is left up to each reader. But it is apparent that the playwright is telling us that expectation and hope are part of the human condition.

The Benefits of Expectation

Expectation has a functional side to it as well. We organize our responses to the future with our expectations. We could not plan tomorrow's shopping, prepare for the predicted storm, put aside money for our daughter's education without anticipating the future. Expectation provides us with a sense of security. It allows us a rough knowledge of what may occur so we are not overwhelmed by events which, out of the blue, might destroy our composure.

The wish component in expectation also has a functional nature. Wishes are affirmations of the future. Lying in a hospital bed suffering pain and discomfort we may despair, but our wishes create for us the possibility that things will improve. They assume a future exists and give us hope. But they are motivators as well. It is often from our wishes that we derive the will to act and the strength to improve and heal ourselves. The inspired story of the dying patient whose unwavering wish for recovery motivates a "spontaneous remission" of symptoms is now part of contemporary folklore. Wishes are acknowledged as powerful medicine by both the shaman and the psychologist.

Imagine a life devoid of wishes. It would be rather bland and dull, like a rainbow of muted color or a stew without seasoning — acceptable but unexciting. Wishes are like the seedlings that miraculously break through the cracks in the concrete, persistently reaching for the sun. One way or another they will find expression, if not in conscious activity then through the mechanism of the unconscious mind. Freud demonstrated nearly ninety years ago that our wishes surface in dreams no matter how we may inhibit them in our daily life. We have only to examine fantasies, verbal errors, handwriting, material choices to see the omnipresent quality of wishes.

The Problems of Investing in Expectations

Expectations are not evil in and of themselves. Our problem really lies in how we relate to them, how important they are to us and how willing we are to modify or surrender them. Those who suffer from chronic disappointment are the same individuals who overinvest in a particular outcome. Their expectations tend to rule them rather than the other way around. They are unwilling and seemingly unable to adapt to the unexpected. Caught in a web of their own making, they cannot see that they struggle against themselves. Most, in fact, will defend the need for their specific expectations as if they could not survive without them. Nothing could be more self-deceiving.

Why do people invest so dearly in expectation? Remember, no one really invests in the *belief* that an outcome will occur. What we invest in is the *wish* for that outcome. After all, if we anticipate enjoying a film and find it is a dud, why not give up the expectation and accept the reality as quickly as possible? The moviegoer who sits through the picture holding fast to a wish for excellence will leave disappointed. His friend who acknowledges the mediocrity of the film and relinquishes his wish will leave early or find some other amusement in the experience.

It is the wish within each expectation that hooks us and maintains our emotional investment. We don't relinquish our hopes easily. They are like small, precious stones held close to the chest as we walk through troubled neighborhoods. They are to be protected and cherished at all costs.

Digging Deeper: The Lifewishes

Wishes are an essential part of everyone's childhood. We more or less grow up with Santa Claus, the Easter Bunny, the Good Fairy, and other inventions of fantasy to which we direct our hopes for childhood rewards and delights. The unbridled imagination of the child can create the most marvelous of possible outcomes. We regard his wishes indulgently as charming reflections of youth. But there is function here as well. Wishing allows the child to make accommodations to a loss of control over external matters. In the first months after birth, the infant is the center of his own universe. His mother not only exists for him but is experienced as part of him. All the simple desires for contact and food appear to be automatically gratified. Gradually, in normal development, the child discovers his mother is not him, but an "other" apart from him. Some of his desires may not be met. Effort is now required to get gratification, and even the best of efforts may fail to bring the child what he wants. Reality has been introduced. The child learns the world is conditional, not always as pleasurable and rewarding as he once experienced it.

Yet the child yearns for the former state of affairs. He cannot recreate the Eden experience in which he was given constant attention and care. Instead, using his imagination he learns to tolerate his loss and the complexities of his future by wishing. He can wish the world to take any form. He can wish his baby sister did not exist, or that his father were a powerful king and he a prince. He can wish for a bugle, an ice cream cone, a dog. Wishing gives him a measure of imagined control and serves to make life more comforting when reality itself may be impoverished or stressful.

Indeed, many of us as adults unconsciously hold to these early wishes for the world to be fair, benevolent, and gratifying. We deny or avoid the harsher realities of human existence as a means — we think — of shielding ourselves from despair. In much the same way as the child, we want life to be easier, relationships more satisfying, work more meaningful. If we look beyond the apparent wish contained in every expectation, we may find a deeper, more encompassing hope. We can call this the "lifewish" because it is a desire for life or our relationship to it to be a particular way. Consider a woman disappointed in the lack of mutual interests and attitudes in her marriage. During their courtship she and her husband seemed so in love that shared values and feelings were not an issue. Now married, they continue to care for each other, but the sense of harmony has been lost and they feel out of sync. She had expected (wished for) their relationship to remain as it had been, but it has changed. The deeper lifewish in this situation is twofold: the desire for life to go on happily ever after and the wish for love alone to sustain a relationship.

Wishing: An Escape into Illusion

The deeper lifewish reflects an exaggeration or minimization of what really exists, in favor of what would really be preferable. It is an escape route from injustice, violence, insignificance, unhappiness. But as long as we want the world to be fair, we cannot help but feel disappointed when it is not. In wishing for the possibility of our own perfection, we are inevitably faced with the disappointment of our limitations. Important as our wishes are to our sense of future, they also create difficulty. When we believe in their possibility, we cannot assess reality properly. It is like watching a magician perform a sleight of hand. In order to believe in the magic we must see only the illusion created. Our perceptions are influenced by our wishes and contradicting information is screened out.

I once knew a man whose avocation was forecasting earthquakes. He predicted about twenty that never materialized. Then, on the twenty-first try, he hit the nail on the head. A small quake was recorded on the seismograph in the same month and in the general vicinity he had predicted. The man was heralded as a prognosticator of some merit. People forgot that twenty times he had forecast the event and twenty times he had been wrong. One coincidence was accepted as proof of his ability. People wanted to believe and so they conveniently disregarded the failed predictions. They filtered out contradictory data in order to make their wish come true.

When we invest in our wishes to the point where naked reality cannot touch us, we are labeled "psychotic" by the mental health profession. Most of us do not qualify. Our level of denial is more modest. If pressed we can see the world clearly. Catastrophic events, death, and disease often shake us into temporary lucidity. But it is relatively easy for us to hide in the lifewishes which had their beginnings in our childhood. These are the fundamental and deeper wishes which reflect our myths and illusions about life. And these wishes are reflected in our expectations. We have invested in them because we are loath to relinquish this deeper world view. To give it up would bring us face to face with sights and scenes we would rather not see. It would require that we confront the demons we have been long avoiding.

Attainable and Unattainable Expectations

Suppose a young track star is disappointed with his latest time for running a mile. The world record is about ten seconds under four minutes, and his time is close but not record-setting. He is disappointed because he had expected that he would set a new world mark in his last race. It may be possible to meet such an expectation if proper action is taken. That is, if the athlete prepares properly, works diligently, and receives good instruction, the anticipated outcome may, in fact, occur. But suppose the young man's disappointment is the result of an expectation that he will run the mile in two minutes, cutting the world record in half. Such an expectation is unreasonable and cannot be satisfied, regardless of action taken.

All expectation exists on a continuum of possibility. On the one end are those attainable with proper action. On the other are those impossible to meet regardless of action taken. To their chagrin many people harbor expectations which are impossible to fulfill, yet they insist on maintaining them. There are others who have expectations attainable only through behavioral change, but they refuse to take the required action. Still others with reasonable expectations assert that no action is necessary or apply the wrong remedy. All these people are doomed to a disappointment of their own making.

To put disappointment in an early grave, we must be ready to surrender our wishful expectations or take extraordinary actions to meet them. Success in this endeavor relies on our ability to assess possibility realistically, independent of the blinding influence of illusional wishes. We must see things the way they really are. This clarity demands from us the personal honesty and courage to challenge our myths and deeper lifewishes around which we have built much of our world view.

Chapter 2

The Roots of Disappointment

One who has never been disappointed is either a fool or a corpse.
— Graffito

Not all disappointments are equal. Some are devastating. Others scarcely seem to matter. It all depends upon the degree of emotional involvement in the failed expectation. The greater the investment, the more severe the disappointment. Two factors determine the strength of that investment: wish and time. The greater the underlying wish for an event to occur, the stronger the pain when it doesn't; witness the canceled wedding or the postponed vacation. Likewise, time increases the level of yearning. The longer we delay, the more urgent our expectation. Common desire held in check becomes sexual passion. Waiting on line to see a play results in heightened interest. But time increases the intensity of expectation only up to a point, after which it begins to fade. Expecting for too long creates tedium. An old Chinese proverb states it simply: "Want a thing long enough and you don't."

We need some way to intelligently categorize disappointment — to distinguish between the feelings in response to a favorite java joint closing for repairs and the realization that your son is not what you hoped he'd be. Arriving at a method for classifying disappointment is a bit like attempting to catalogue sand on a windy beach. It's everywhere to be found — in the most majestic locations and in the pants leg — but is one grain very different from another? Look closely. Even sand may be divided according to color, coarseness, and density. On examination, we can distinguish four types of disappointment: simple, chronic, developmental, and socially induced.

Simple Disappointment

This is the single, isolated experience of disappointment that accompanies us through our daily existence as we encounter the empty aspirin bottle, the inedible dinner, the uncooperative spouse. It may further be divided into two types: "lightweight" disappointments most people could do without but accept as a consequence of living, and those significant, deep experiences of disappointment that wound and require recovery time, like the failure to get the job you really wanted or the breakup of a love affair.

Simple disappointments do not show a pattern. Each is different and there is no element of predictability. They are the result of faulty judgment, unrealistic expectations, exaggerated hopes, and chance. It is with these isolated experiences of disappointment that we are best acquainted. They are inevitable — by-products of the human capacity to fantasize and wish. Into every life some disappointment must fall. Most of us have few problems dealing with lightweight disappointments; we make adjustments without complaint. We are willing to concede our wishes once in a while. More significant disappointments, however, elicit emotional pain because our investment in them is so much greater. Yet even this kind of distress is manageable, since it will pass with time. All simple disappointments are subject to modification through insight and behavioral intervention. Whether we feel pain or successfully avoid it depends on our willingness to understand the nature of disappointment.

Chronic Disappointment

Far more difficult to eliminate are the chronic disappointments that drag on for extended periods and are repeated time and again. These are predictable experiences that follow a habitual routine. I have called such patterns "disappointment styles," because they are determined by enduring character traits which reflect the emotional history of the individual. If someone is continually and repeatedly disappointed in her children, job, or lot in life, we may assume there is something in her personality that produces these chronic feelings.

Since disappointments are generally felt one at a time and memories of unhappy experience can be repressed, the chronically disappointed frequently fail to perceive the pattern of disillusionment in their own lives, and are thus helpless to bring an end to their deflated feelings.

Put another way, chronically disappointed individuals don't learn from past experience. The feedback mechanism that enables the human being to avoid stepping in the same quicksand twice is in need of repair. The narcissist who believes he is entitled to special treatment, for example, will be disappointed when he is assigned to an undistinguished office like his coworkers'. Yet he does not learn from this experience. On the contrary, that very same afternoon he is disappointed again when the boss vetoes his request for special time off, and once more that evening when the maitre d' keeps him waiting in line with everyone else.

Whether out of fear, disapproval, or anxiety, those who repeatedly experience disappointment have a psychological history that has produced expectations that are unrealistic, too absolute, too high or low. They need to readjust those expectations, but forces in their personality prevent them from doing so. Consider those individuals with impossibly high internal expectations who mistakenly believe that such standards are necessary to keep them from sinking into mediocrity. Underneath their impossible demands for excellence, they suffer deep insecurity. They would rather experience the repeated disappointment provoked by their perfectionism than relinquish the rigidly high expectations which they believe keep them from becoming second-rate. The college student who refuses to submit a paper unless it is absolutely letter-perfect or the ad executive who demands that every client presentation be flawless illustrate this self-defeating style.

Habitually disappointed individuals feel depressed and lackluster most of the time. The experience of hope repeatedly followed by letdown is an emotional roller coaster that takes the joy and lightness out of life. Stuck in a morass from which they are seemingly powerless to escape, they feel frustrated and helpless. As long as they remain prisoners of their own psychological history, they will continue to repeat the patterns that create disappointment.

Developmental Disappointment

As we pass through the various stages of life from infancy to old age, we find that certain disappointments are characteristic of a particular time of development. The young child, for example, innocent and unworldly, can be disappointed by virtually any event. He sees no limits on possibility. Life is mysterious and magical. Expectations are boundless. Disappointment is, therefore, frequent and traumatic. His mother, in her mid-thirties, is just beginning to fathom that many of her plans for the future will not be realized. Her alternatives are shrinking, and she must make either/or choices. Her disappointments are born of the adult developmental stage through which she is passing. Her father, in turn, must confront the disappointment of lost opportunities and plans never completed. He is faced with age-old questions: "Is that all there is?" "How would I do it differently the second time around?" "Is life fundamentally disappointing?" Each stage of the human drama brings its own disappointments as aspiration collides with reality.

These developmental disappointments, so devastating in their impact, are important learning experiences. Contained within each is a challenge to our illusions about being. Rather than ignore or avoid them, we would do well to employ them to help us through the lifelong process of maturation. Like an austere teacher, birch switch in hand, they rap our knuckles with hard fact. They say, "You cannot live forever; opportunities are fleeting; life is short; we never get all that we want." They readjust our view of things by teaching us about the limits of possibility and the nature of life. The child cannot have every gratification. The octogenarian has only limited time remaining. And so forth. Developmental disappointment impels us to give up our dreams and make the most of what is. By doing so, we put our energy into living life instead of regretting its nature.

Socially Induced Disappointment

The mood of the nation — the collective feelings of optimism or desperation — is affected by powerful economic forces beyond individual control. Interest and employment rates, inflation levels, and stock market growth directly influence levels of personal satisfaction. When times are good, people generally feel optimistic about their personal lives. Less apparent are the social forces which impact our attitudes and perceptions. Advertising, television, and movies exercise subtle sway. They spoon-feed us on their brand of fantastic expectation and dispose us to disappointment when those dreams don't pan out in real life.

We are impressionable animals highly attuned to the variety of messages sent out to us through the advertising media. The constant barrage of gratuitous commercials is one of the hazards of life in the twentieth century. It is inescapable. Beautiful young men and women stroll leisurely through the woods to the background music of a dozen violins in order to induce us to buy an aftershave lotion or motor oil. No cares, no responsibilities, no oil on the fingertips. Such ideal representations suggest that purchase of the product will do the same for us. What's more, they persuade us that acquisition itself is salutary and meaningful.

In choosing to present imagined visions of life based on familiar myths such as the triumph of the little guy or the power of love, Hollywood and the television networks cater to maudlin, commercial tastes. Nothing fills the theaters like an updated morality play or a romance disguised in futuristic costume. The public will pay money to see them. What the public will not pay to see are films that portray the shadow side of reality. Few want to watch a slice of life. They prefer to escape it.

The themes and format of television and motion pictures affect our perceptions in much the same way as advertising. They encourage our own personal myths — which were in part created by the media — while inflating and romanticizing expectation. In presenting a world of illusion, the entertainment industry fills our unconscious with word pictures and ideas ungrounded in realism. By comparison, daily life seems two-dimensional and disappointing.

Socially induced disappointment may result from major economic and political forces or from the covert influence of the media in our lives. Yet it hardly matters whether the White House, Madison Avenue, or Hollywood sets the conditions for feelings of disillusionment. The real issue is how to stay clear of these forces, a task that just may prove impossible. Perhaps the words of philosopher Alan Watts offer a solution: "Be in the world but not of it."

Is Disappointment Destiny?

As we consider the roots of disappointment, the inexorable question surfaces: Is the nature of life disappointing? A friend put it to me directly. "Why bother to look at specific disappointments? Life itself is pretty disappointing."

I asked him to elaborate, and he replied, "You're trying to solve the riddle of disappointment as if you could prevent it or help people to move through it, but what if the experience of life is intrinsically disappointing? What if life is not all it's cracked up to be? What if living itself is disenchanting?"

It was a jolting thought. Was I running around like a battle-crazed medic applying psychological Band-Aids and gauze to a problem that was simply inherent in life? Was repetitive disappointment built into a universal plan? If so, my remedies would be as effective as aspirin on left-handedness. Soberly, I thought more about my friend's observation. For some reason I remembered an old joke from my youth:

A homely woman goes to a matchmaker who extols the virtues of a certain man seeking a spouse. "He's rich, kind, and looks just like Cary Grant," insists the matchmaker. Enticed by the prospect, the woman agrees to meet her prospective suitor in a cafe the next evening. She arrives early, barely containing her excitement. At the prescribed moment, an old man shuffles in and sits down next to her. In her disappointment she bursts out crying. "You don't look a thing like Cary Grant." "You know something else?" he replies. "You don't resemble Gina Lollobrigida!"

Disappointment is a function of expectation. And in selling her suitors on each other, the matchmaker had created impossible expectations. To the question "Is life itself disappointing?" we must in turn ask, "What did you expect?" Expect life to be fair, good to triumph over evil, the dead to rise again, miracles to save you, the wronged to gain redress, and you will feel constant disappointment. Life may be inherently too short or dissatisfying, but it is not intrinsically disappointing, since that condition is determined exclusively by what you anticipate. It is how you view life, not life itself, that creates disappointment.

"Don't expect Cary Grant," I said to my friend, "and you won't be disappointed when Woody Allen shows up."

"You have an interesting point," said my friend, "but you're not considering the structure of life. As children we live in our imagination, with visions of endless choice and possibility. Life is like a huge menu. A child wants to eat everything it sees. We always ask children, 'What do you want to be when you grow up?' as if anything they choose is possible. We collude with their visions. And they say, 'I want to be a fireman, a brain surgeon, the first woman on the moon.' Anything. They believe anything is possible."

"But that's just the innocence of childhood," I retorted. "When they grow up they have to adjust to the world."

"That's just the point. The nature of life is to begin with endless possibility and as the years go by all possibility diminishes. Time shrinks possibility!"

"Some of our dreams come true," I countered. "In fact, it is only as adults that we can accomplish what we imagine. Children have to be satisfied with wishes only."

"Maybe it's true that you may reach a few of your dreams in adulthood, but not many, compared to what you've imagined. To a child, the future is a vast expanse. But as you get older, time and energy — what you need to meet your expectations — keep diminishing. At thirty, you see that life is too short to achieve perhaps 50 percent of what you had wanted. At forty the figure gets even smaller, and so on. To make matters worse, you have less energy as you age. Managing a household, earning a living, and raising children are exhausting, even with an abundant supply of energy. Add to this the psychological responsibilities of adulthood and the physical problems of an aging body and you have a very heavy burden indeed.

"You start from a single point looking out at endless possibility. Your expectations are limitless. As you live on, fewer and fewer of those expectations are met. That's why life is by nature disappointing. You begin with promise and end with the cold, hard limitations of reality."

I knew my friend was at least partially right, but where he saw inevitable disappointment in the structure of life, I saw something else.

"It's true what you say," I replied, "but you fail to take one human factor into account: adaptability. Life may be an ellipse; possibility may funnel into limited reality. But if you know this will occur, you can make adjustments. The observation of a fact changes that fact. It may not be possible to eliminate disappointments, yet you can reduce them to a manageable level by accepting the natural life sequence you have just described. That means acknowledging that all your dreams cannot come true, and that human beings age and change. Maturation is a process of learning to accept life as it is. Repeated disappointment is a failure to accept the world without qualification. If you're willing to accept it as it is, then life does not have to be disappointing. There's enough excitement and wonder in living to justify relinquishing false hope."

Death and Taxes

Awareness of the elliptical nature of life gives us a perspective that prevents disappointment from getting out of hand, but it does not help us to eliminate it entirely. In later chapters, we will learn ways to reduce the level of disappointment in our lives and to deal effectively with significant experiences of letdown as they occur. We will explore methods for using disappointment to enrich our experience and prevent us from suffering greater disillusionment. But we must recognize that, like death and taxes, some disappointment is inevitable, a by-product of the foibles of human nature — the timeless patterns and quirks that are universal and historical. Embedded in civilization, these patterns are so commonplace that we are scarcely aware of them. Yet they explain why disappointment may shadow every human experience.

Taking Things for Granted

A friend recently told me of his plans to move for the third time in as many years. He lived in a lovely beach house with a magnificent view of the ocean. A labyrinth of hiking trails strewn with wild irises and poppies were at his front door. I asked why he might leave such a beautiful setting.

"Oh, I'm tired of it," he responded indifferently. "It was great when I first moved in, but now it's just the same old thing. I can't see it anymore."

"I can't see it anymore." How accurate the statement. He failed to notice the ocean. He walked by the flowers without so much as a glance. He thought of his home as merely a place to lay down his head. Living in paradise, he might just as well have resided at the city dump. Nine people out of ten would have jumped at the opportunity to rent my friend's house, yet he did not appreciate its virtues.

Human beings have a curious capacity to take things for granted. The most exquisite diamond loses its luster with familiarity. The most compatible intimate becomes boring. Miracles like the daily sunrise fail to astonish because they're commonplace! Repetition and time dull our sense of wonder. A favorite record played over and over becomes monotonous and dreary. Filet mignon consumed every day loses its savoriness. Even the fragrance of a rose stops arousing our sense receptors after only a few seconds.

We endow novelty with powers and attributes that it does not really possess. When a thing becomes familiar to us, the mystery we have projected onto it is lost. We see it without the overlay of our imaginings. A new boy in class inspires fantasy in the schoolgirl until she gets to know him and he becomes just another kid. The young employee attributes maternal qualities to his older supervisor until he finds she is critical and unkind.

The irony in this idiosyncrasy of human character is that we are disappointed by the very things that used to excite us. The once new job, sexual partner, or leisure activity is now tedious. We feel let down rather than uplifted. Disappointment is a consequence of our expectation that an object or event will continue to provide us with stimulation regardless of how constant our contact. Unless we adjust our expectations accordingly, we will continue to feel deflated.

Anticipate boredom! But is this really a serious solution? Let me suggest another alternative: Maintain a fresh perspective on the commonplace by living life with contrast. If my friend had spent time away from his ocean home, he would have returned to it with "new" eyes. He would have seen it again as he did the first time. Some people take long vacations for just this purpose — to provide the distance necessary to see their life anew and appreciate it. Absence makes the heart grow fonder. We value what we don't have. We take for granted what we do.

If the world were all red, we would not even know that red existed. Since everything would be that color, we would simply assume it was the nature of things. Introduce contrast in the form of blue, and we suddenly become aware that red exists. Now we can see it because it can be compared to something else. It is contrast that provides us with the antidote to taking things for granted and feeling disappointment. As the Chinese philosopher Lao Tzu wrote 2,500 years ago, "Under heaven all can see beauty as beauty only because there is ugliness. All can know good as good only because there is evil."

Missing the Present Moment

After their children had left home, Amy and Richard, a professional couple in their mid-fifties, decided to take a trip around the world. Having lived in the same place for thirty years, they found the idea of globetrotting exciting and romantic. Here was an opportunity to view firsthand the cultural and natural wonders they had read about in novels and travelogues. They planned the entire trip carefully and thoughtfully, educating themselves about local customs, currencies, and places of interest. They studied languages, investigated climates, and planned extensive itineraries. Armed with the appropriate intestinal medications, they boarded the airplane and flew off to the Orient.

When they arrived at their first stop, they were excited and nervous. Hardly noticing the sea of humanity directly before them, they hurried madly from one place to another, determined to see everything in the guidebook. Each night they returned to their hotel tired and irritable. They weren't really having a good time, but they attributed it to jet lag. The second stop was much the same. Every day was a faultless replication of the itinerary

planned back in the States. Something was n
neither of them could identify it. In spite of tł
settled into a routine and ignored their disco
was so much to see and photograph.

On their return months later, they felt fatigueɑ ⸱
surprisingly relieved. But then a puzzling phenomenon occurred.
As they talked to their friends and family, they saw their vacation
in a new light. It became an adventure, a thrilling experience.
Through the distorting lens of memory, they had reframed it as
satisfying and meaningful. The emptiness of the real experience
had been filtered out. The vacation was a great success when seen
from this perspective. Anticipating and remembering the event
was better than the experience itself.

This sort of behavior might be called living in the "before and
after." Instead of experiencing the rich tableaux of life unfolding
before them, Amy and Richard were preoccupied with following
the demands of an itinerary prepared three months before from a
distance of ten thousand miles. They felt they were missing
something and they were: the present moment as experienced
through their five senses.

Living in the moment —what Richard Alpert (aka Ram Dass)
calls "being here now" — means intentional awareness of self and
situation. This is *not* a high mystical state that requires fasting or
meditation, but it is nevertheless difficult to achieve. With the
laser-pace of modern life and all the distractions, stimulations and
frustrations of trying to do too much in too little time, many
people get through the day by *not* paying attention. They eat
without tasting, listen without hearing, look without seeing, very
often preoccupied with what they did this morning or what they
have to do later. If we had asked Amy or Richard, "Did you enjoy
your trip?" their honest answer might have been, "We didn't really
notice!"

Preoccupation with tomorrow or yesterday prevents us from feeling the satisfaction (or discomfort) of instantaneous experience. It blocks us from the immediacy of our own lives. A brisk morning walk by a clear mountain stream holds no thrill to a hiker ruminating about the business meeting last Tuesday. The engrossed manager is missing the encounter with the natural world — walking, smelling, observing, feeling. Consciousness of the temporal moment — "bare attention," in Buddhist terminology — is fundamental to a satisfying and healthy life.

Much of what we call disappointment relates to our inability to fully experience the "now." Without awareness of the present we merely swallow experience without savoring it. Even the most favored delicacy will disappoint the palate if it is not given sufficient attention. Living in the moment is a prescription for satisfaction as old as the Bible. King Solomon declared: "A man hath no better thing under the sun than to eat, and to drink, and to be merry"; the Roman poet Horace asserted: *"Carpe diem, quam minimum credula postero"* (Seize the present, trust tomorrow e'en as little as you may); and the American poet, Longfellow:

> *Trust no future, howe'er pleasant*
> *Let the dead Past bury its dead!*
> *Act, act in the living Present!*
> *Heart within and God o'erhead.*

As children, we are absorbed in the present moment without much concern for future or past events. Over time, the "cerebral wiring" becomes more complex and we find ourselves absorbed in other concerns. This change is necessary and inevitable. There are lessons to be learned from the past and problems to anticipate in the future.

Continual present-centeredness may be more an ideal than a natural condition in technological society. It takes practice and awareness to achieve it, and it is doubtful if any but the highly disciplined could manage it without interruption. Even if we could, it is questionable whether our full interests would be served. Still, we can strive for a better balance between living in the "before and after" and the "here and now."

To live in the moment, thereby reducing our predisposition to disappointment, we must ask with regularity three orienting questions of ourselves. "At this moment: What is it I feel? What is it I sense? What is it I want?" The answers will focus us on the present and put us in better touch with ourselves.

Faultless Fantasy

The capacity to contemplate great things, to imagine perfection, valiant victories, and marvelous futures suggests an inevitable confrontation with disappointment. Our imaginations have no limit. The power we have to form mental pictures then turn them upside down and inside out, embellish them with brilliant color, create three dimensions, happy endings and impossible outcomes would make any special effects genius salivate with envy. Eden, Shangri-La, Arcadia, Neverland, Atlantis, Laputa, and the Big Rock Candy Mountain represent only a few of the utopias that have captivated the human heart in former generations. Fantasy is faultless. All defects are removed by the dreamer.

But real life, well, that's another matter. Reality is filled with blisters and pockmarks. It is limited by the physical laws of nature. Although sometimes difficult to define — parapsychology gives us cause to wonder — the perimeters of possibility are generally accepted. Life is finite. Our bodies require sleep, food, and water to survive. The sun sets every day. And so forth. The discrepancy between what we can imagine life to be and how it is lived can be fertile ground for disappointment.

My friend, Glenn, decided to build his own house, something he had always dreamed of doing. He pictured himself, hammer in hand, constructing the walls that would shelter his family from wind and cold. The sweat of his brow and the effort of his labor would be the foundation of this new structure. Like the frontier pioneers before him, he would literally construct his future.

You might guess what happened. The experience of building did not quite meet the relished expectation. Instead, Glenn found himself enmeshed in the prosaic details of building codes, community architectural standards, and septic tank regulations. The pioneer vision was replaced by sore thumbs and a slipped disc. Reality had once again supplanted fantasy; disappointment was the consequence.

Imagination is a gift of mind that cannot be adequately treasured. It would not be unfair to suggest that all human progress is its consequence. That does not mean it has no shadow. Samuel Johnson is reputed to have said, "Were it not for imagination a man would be as happy in the arms of a chambermaid as of a duchess." Here is precisely the problem. Reality can't measure up to what the mind is capable of contemplating.

The words of a seventeenth-century Archbishop of Canterbury describe this very human dilemma:

> In our pursuit of the things of this world, we usually prevent enjoyment by expectation; we anticipate our happiness, and eat out the heart and sweetness of worldly pleasures by delightful forethoughts of them; so that when we come to possess them, they do not answer the expectation, or satisfy the desires which were raised about them, and they vanish into nothing.

Empowering Objects

A husband and wife hope that buying a sailboat will help their faltering marriage by giving them a common interest. The boat not only fails to repair their damaged relationship, but becomes a convenient object to fight over. A college sophomore wants a new sports car to enhance his image and combat inner feelings of inadequacy. After buying it, he discovers that even at 120 m.p.h. he feels bad about himself

We often expect acquisition to provide magical remedies. We imagine objects have the power to furnish happiness and deeper satisfaction. As the struggling couple and insecure college student soon realize, their solutions do little more than direct attention away from more significant dilemmas. The problems remain.

The issue is further complicated by the symbolic meaning we attach to particular objects. We see prestige, security, power, and respect in the procurement of material goods. The expensive automobile, the duplex on Park Avenue, the vintage wine all represent more than the possessions themselves. We imagine our association with them gives us standing and increases our merit. We hope somehow to be endowed with all the attributes which we project onto these objects. Like primitive people in the hill country of some distant land, we ascribe miraculous influence to the wooden thingumajig. Only ours are sold in the downtown department store. A designer suit will win us admiration. A prized fragrance will make us irresistible Simply by obtaining such articles, we hope to capture their authority.

Of course, these expectations must end in disaster. Material acquisitions may make our lives easier and more comfortable, but they don't solve emotional problems or provide deeper satisfactions. Yet we continue to gather up and surround ourselves with possessions like squirrels preparing for the coming winter. We are particularly attracted to objects we can't possess. Offer a child A or B, but under no circumstances C, and the choice is a foregone conclusion. Adults are no different. They ascribe greater merit to the unobtainable and devalue what is more easily acquired. So predictable is this behavior that advertisers use it to manufacture interest in their products. By suggesting exclusivity, they increase interest.

Whatever the reasons for our attraction to material trappings, it is important to keep our expectations regarding acquisition within the bounds of reality. Unto themselves, objects have no value beyond their immediate usefulness. When we expect them to help us avoid suffering or provide deeper satisfaction and meaning, we will always be disappointed. A new pair of shoes offers only a temporary remedy for depression. We would do better to address our problems directly.

Fault Focusing

Out for a Sunday drive, a young couple happens upon a house for sale. They wander into the place and two hours later reemerge having inspected it from attic to cellar. "I love it," she says. "Let's make an offer today." "I hate it," comes the reply. "It needs a family room, the backyard doesn't get any sun, the decking needs to be replaced, and there's not enough storage." Sounds typical, right? Not exactly. This couple's been looking for a house for five years and it's always the same story. She's receptive, he's negative. No matter how desirable the house he always focuses on the flaws.

Some people are practiced at seeing only problems or defects. They zero in on what's wrong or missing and don't seem to notice observable attributes and virtues. Even when these are acknowledged, their importance is minimized even as imperfections are exaggerated. In this case it's the perceived deficiencies of houses, but it might just as well be the failings of friends, films, or females. Fault focusing transcends specific circumstances. It is a style of collecting and interpreting information. Imagine looking at the countless stars that light up the night sky and feeling disappointed because the visibility isn't as keen as the night before. That's what it's like to be a critic. You miss everything but the flaw. Eventually you feel that life itself doesn't measure up. But it's not life that's the problem. It's the inability to appreciate what's wonderful and marvelous about life.

Focusing on faults is a defense against suffering letdown. If you don't have illusions, the rationalization goes, you won't feel letdown when flaws are discovered. But the solution becomes the problem when nothing is ever seen as good enough. Then disappointment is a constant companion.

What's missing is the capacity to appreciate. Appreciation with a capital "A" is a sensibility — a receptiveness that allows one to see beauty where others see ugliness, value where others see uselessness, purpose where others see chaos. It's what enables the poet to rhyme and the rest of us to feel happiness. The young are well endowed with it and ironically take it for granted. But as with so many things that disappear with time, this one becomes more precious as experience dulls our capacity for wonder and awe. We need appreciation to balance the critic within us.

The Deception of Appearances

In my clinical practice, I happened to be seeing two women who held similar sales jobs in the same company. They knew each other only superficially, but their relationship was cordial and friendly. Susan had occasion to remark how much she liked Pat, emphasizing what a happy, good-humored person she seemed to be. Pat, on the other hand, was taken with Susan's knowledge of herself. She thought of her acquaintance as "really in touch." The impressions Susan and Pat had of each other were the antitheses of what I knew to be true. Susan was an avoider, someone who would resort to almost any ploy to evade recognition of her true motivation. Pat wore a mask of pleasantness to conceal her discontent and sadness.

People are often deceived by appearances. They mistake form for substance, assuming that what is displayed is a reflection of what exists below the surface. To complicate matters further, all of us play a game called "putting the best foot forward." This is a euphemism that encompasses a range of behavior from affectation to outright duplicity. We try to fool people into thinking we are better, richer, stronger, more loving than we actually are.

In spite of the fact that we're all in on this game, many of us seem to forget the other person is playing too. When we see someone who is "cool, calm, and collected," we often assume that the individual has no personal problems and is able to handle adversity without difficulty.

In the clinical setting, it is common for patients with low self esteem to compare themselves with others. Rarely is the evaluation accurate. Patients are all too familiar with their own shortcomings. They do not possess parallel information about others. As a result, they contrast their worst traits with the public image of strangers. And, of course, they end up disappointed in themselves.

Our society places great stress on appearances. Nowhere is this better illustrated than in the marketplace, where display is everything. American automobiles have always been long on exterior design and short on function. Only in recent years has international competition forced a shift in priorities. So much money is spent on packaging consumer goods that the process is an industry in itself. The attractive label, the eye-catching container, the intriguing trademark are considered vital to successful marketing. In many cases the package is more important and more costly than the product. The general rule is, "If it looks good, it sells good!"

Image and style are paramount in the political arena as well. Issues generally run second to presentation of self. What matters is the tone of voice, the choice of homily, the hair and jacket cut. Does the candidate look and act presidential? Is she a winner? Does he command respect? Social critics warn that we sell politicians at election time the way we merchandise washing machines — in thirty-second spots praising the virtues of the product. "He's a family man." "She's one of us." "He cares." The trend is to ignore the issues — certainly the most fundamental aspect of any campaign — and focus on personality. The candidate's winning smile counts more than her position on defense spending.

Disappointment and the deception of appearances are inextricably wedded. Eventually we discover that the candidate is just another person subject to the compromising pressures of political life. Or the new friend who seemed so easygoing initially is really compulsive and critical. All that glitters is not gold, is not even metal, but plastic! When we form judgements and expectations on the basis of outward show without consideration of their inner nature, we are walking a path that leads directly to disillusionment. It is important for human beings, who are so vulnerable to bright lights and tinsel, to remember that form itself can be deceptive. What we see on the surface is not necessarily what we find underneath.

Chapter 3

The Anatomy of Disappointment

The movements of expression give vividness and energy to our spoken words. They reveal the thoughts and intentions of others more truly than do words, which may be falsified.... These results follow partly from the intimate relation which exists between almost all emotions and their outward manifestation....

— Charles Darwin

The Six Stages of Disappointment

What does it feel like to be disappointed? I asked my nephew, the screenwriter/computer genius, that question and received an instantaneous reply. "You're playing *Myst*, and you've been at it for a few days working really hard, and you're about to solve the final mystery when your hard drive crashes and you lose all the info." I've never played the game, but I understood the metaphor. The more intense the desire, the greater the expectation. And when the desire is at its peak and you're already planning the celebration, you get the bad news and groan in disbelief: "Could this really be happening? I was so close." A half-dozen or so exasperated thoughts run through your mind at rapid speed. But all you really notice is the end consequence: disappointment. Let's look more closely at the workings of this process.

Suppose you have applied for a job with a high-flying tech firm. The salary is double what you're earning now and there are travel opportunities, a large office, and an expense account. The possibility of further advancement is good. Your potential boss is due for promoion, and her job will be up for grabs. Your interview went well. They liked your resume and emphasized that you're one of their top candidates. Now it's call back time. Naturally, you've got butterflies — more like migrating geese — in your stomach. The phone rings. It's the recruiter: "I'm sorry to have to..." Your mouth drops. You feel terrible. Although you had told yourself not to "count your chickens," you really had expected to be hired. After all, you were one of their top choices.

Your first reaction is simply alarm — an "Oh!" response like an electric current running through the body. You are jolted by the delivery of discouraging news and your physiology is reacting by reflex. It's an unpleasant feeling, an orienting reaction to help you further process the information to follow. And it is quickly replaced by a sense of disbelief. You don't really accept the truth of the caller's statements although she couldn't be more coolly precise. She's told you the bad news but, for a few brief seconds at least, her words have not been fully acknowledged. You may think to yourself, "I can't believe this." Or "I can't accept this." Or "Is this really how it's going to be?" Your mind's rejection is similar to the experience of purging spoiled food. The body says, "Get rid of it. It can't be processed." Likewise, the mind responds, "I don't want to process it." The denial defense cannot be maintained for long, however. In the face of indisputable reality, the bitter truth seeps in. Your thoughts turn in another direction. Perhaps you think about how hard you prepared for the interview, how you had to buy a new suit or rehearse for several hours.

Suddenly the injustice of it all strikes home. You're angry. You want to protest: "The nerve of those people. They don't know what they're losing." You might even take the whole affair personally and feel rejected and hurt.

Eventually you begin to feel a sense of loss. The objective fact sinks in. You lose energy. You feel depressed. You'd like to withdraw to the safe confines of your bedroom and sleep away the next two days. You think to yourself. "I'll never find another job as good.... All that effort and I'm back where I started.... If only I had been hired." The realization of loss grows keener and you may find it hard to put it out of your mind. Dwelling on it produces feelings of resignation. The situation seems hopeless. Life is suddenly bleak. All opportunities lead to a dead end, so why even try? Perhaps you even consider the undermining thought: *There's something the matter with me.* You go to bed but sleep doesn't come easily. The next day is plagued by listlessness and intermittent feelings of purposelessness and resignation.

Many people seem to get stuck in this particular phase of the disappointment process. Dwelling on the failed expectation, they exaggerate its meaning and importance. Suddenly their whole world appears to have depended on this one specific outcome. All perspective is lost.

Time heals most wounds if we allow it. Several days later, failure to get the job no longer seems so important. You have accepted the unfortunate news and moved through your disappointment. But rather than feel elated or relieved, you experience a curious absence of feeling. Other aspects of your life now seem more pressing. The disappointment fades into memory.

Until now you may have considered disappointment to be only a feeling, a specific emotion characterized by loss. After all, we commonly say, "I feel disappointed." However, it's more accurate to think of disappointment as a process broader in scope.

Like the experience of grief, it has phases and direction. We might say disappointment is the struggle involved in moving from the failure of a desired outcome through the pain of loss to an acceptance of new circumstances.

Looking at our example again, we can identify six stages.

1. Expectation
2. Expectation Lost
3. Alarm
4. Resistance
5. Loss and Resignation
6. Acceptance

Admittedly, this is a rather neat and tidy model of the disappointment experience. Daily living rarely proceeds this clearly and simply. In actuality, the resistance stage may follow the loss rather than precede it. Anger, hurt, and self-pity may flow out of the disappointed feeling, or the phases may be experienced in combination without clear delineation. But in general, the six stages portray the comprehensive process of moving through disappointment. Most of us will find it a useful road map when trying to gain our bearings in the midst of a disappointing experience.

Disappointment as Grief

In her well-known book *On Death and Dying,* Dr. Elisabeth Kubler-Ross identifies five stages through which the dying person moves in order to finally accept impending death: denial and isolation, anger, bargaining, depression, acceptance. These stages are markedly similar to those of the disappointment process. Denial and anger are early reactions in both cycles. Depression corresponds to the loss and resignation phase. Acceptance serves as the final resolution. Why should the reaction to disappointment appear analogous to the profound response to death? Surely the permanence and finality of the latter cannot be compared with the sometimes trivial nature of disappointment.

There is a natural progression of internal events when human beings confront any significant loss — no matter what the nature. We move through grief in a particular way. Most psychologists agree that there are no shortcuts. Disappointment involves a specific type of grief. Disappointed persons mourn for the death of a desire rather than for the loss of a parent or spouse. They had expected good weather for the celebration, but it rained instead. They anticipated their child would be accepted at Harvard, but she was refused admission. The significance of the loss may be small compared to the end of life, but it is loss nonetheless. To move to an acceptance of the new state of affairs requires predictable and patterned psychological maneuvers. Denial, anger, and resignation are preconditions necessary to fully absorb the new reality. For this reason, although death is far more tangible and momentous than disappointment, the human reaction is quite similar.

Yet logic tells us there is something unsound about comparing death with disappointment. Are we measuring apples against oranges? Not quite. It is more like comparing types of oranges or, in this case, types of losses. The differences are apparent. First, death is permanent and irreversible. Disappointment has no finality. What is lost can usually be gained at another place and time. And even if it cannot, the process of expecting continues. Unlike death, disappointment is only a setback on life's journey. Second, death is a concrete loss, whereas disappointment is merely the failure of an idea. Third, the magnitude of death dwarfs disappointment, even in chronic form. The existentialist philosophers call it the ultimate "boundary situation" — an experience that forces us to confront our own lives and place them in new perspective. Disappointment can help us to better understand the limits of possibility, but it rarely motivates a massive shift in the way we view our lives.

Disappointment as Stress

The mind and body function together as a whole. What we experience in our bodies affects what we think, and our thoughts have the power to produce physiological changes. Suppose you're meeting an old lover for lunch and you're anxious about the encounter. You wonder whether he'll still be attracted to you or if he carries resentment from the past. Such thoughts produce reactions in your body. Your breathing is shallow, you feel your heart beating rapidly, your hands are cold and sweaty. These alarming sensations in turn produce greater nervousness, more apprehension and doubt. Now you're certain the meeting is a bad idea. Perhaps he has an ulterior motive or wants something from you. Both mind and body are simultaneously involved in the discomfort. The mental event is a physical event. When an individual is disappointed, the same sort of dual reaction can be detected. Disappointment may begin in the mind, but it soon produces effects in the body.

Anyone who has ever been repeatedly disappointed knows that the experience is exhausting and debilitating. We might, in fact, call it stress-inducing, because the effort required to cope wears us down. Stress is credited with a role in many prominent psychological and physical problems, including peptic ulcer, colitis, bronchial asthma, hypertension, enuresis, migraine headache, general sexual dysfunction, insomnia, alcoholism, and a variety of neurotic and psychotic problems. Roughly 50 to 80 percent of all disease falls into this category of psychosomatic illness — disorders which are associated with or exacerbated by psychological factors.

Does disappointment contribute to this long list of ailments? Certainly, combined with other adversity, it increases a person's overall level of stress. By itself, however, most psychologists would probably rank it as only a minor nuisance. As a matter of fact, on the widely used *Social Readjustment Scale,* which assigns numerical values to stress-inducing life events, disappointment is not even listed.

But suppose our earlier example of disappointment occurred in another context. You've been out of work for six months and are feeling some desperation because of precarious finances and significant loss to your self-esteem. In such a tight situation, the disappointment of not being hired would indeed create higher levels of stress. The unmet expectation might well be felt as a telling and final blow. The more desperate the context, the greater its destructive influence.

There is other evidence to indicate that the stress of chronic disappointment can produce physical and psychological problems. One of the most powerful experiences of disappointment is the one suffered by the repeatedly impotent male and his sexual partner. Nothing is more frustrating than continued unsuccessful attempts at coitus. Because anticipation and desire must necessarily be at high levels, the letdown created by failure to successfully complete the sexual act can be devastating. The male may feel frustrated and helpless, his self-esteem dealt a grievous blow. Partners usually feel equally distraught and disappointed. They may think of themselves as undesirable or unattractive. Eventually, and often without discussion, both lovers collude in the avoidance of sexual contact. Neither wants to be disappointed yet another time. The scenario becomes a chronic cycle of expectation — disappointment — hopelessness, followed again by expectation.... It is an obvious example of how prolonged disappointment immobilizes and defeats.

Studies at Loyola University's Sexual Dysfunction Clinic suggest that the price of this disappointment is high. Sixty-two percent of the sexual partners of males with erection difficulties developed their own sexual problems over time. Many reported physical symptoms, including chronic backache and lower abdominal pain. Others became depressed and complained of feelings of rejection and sexual unattractiveness. Clearly, the relationship between chronic disappointment and the development of pathology is a direct one.

If disappointment works internally to produce unfavorable consequences for health and well-being, its more obvious effects on the anatomy of the disillusioned individual are also observable. Chronic disappointment is recorded in the body over time, revealed in posture and muscular-tension patterns. Less obvious are transitory disappointments which may be intentionally masked. Human beings are quite proficient at hiding their inner feelings at least temporarily, and may reveal no outward appearance of letdown. Yet without these learned checks on expression, disappointment would likely be as easy to detect as it is in children who are more demonstrative than their acculturated parents.

The Physiology of Disappointment

In recent years there has been renewed interest in the interaction of the mind and body. For generations medical schools emphasized the Cartesian duality of body and mind as separate and distinct entities. Today it is generally accepted that the mind influences, if not the etiology, then the course and intensity of many diseases. Studies show that even killers like cancer and heart disease are highly influenced by attitude and belief.

Dean Ornish who has done pioneer research on the role of diet and heart disease, believes that helping people express their feelings and attend to their relationships can change the biochemistry that predisposes them to illness. He cites many studies that confirm this. Women who answered "yes" to the question, "do you feel isolated?" were 3-1/2 times as likely to die of breast, uterine or ovarian cancer than those who said "no." Men who did not feel loved by their wives suffered 50 percent more angina over a five year period than those who felt loved.

Paul Eckman at the University of California, San Francisco has demonstrated that individuals who grimace, frown, scowl and otherwise manifest affective facial expressions are actually influencing their biochemistry in the process. Smiling, for example, is therapeutic and appears to release the body's own natural "feel good" chemicals: beta endorphins.

How does disappointment affect anatomy and biochemistry? Think of the body as a large piece of clay molded by experience and genetic factors. The muscles of the body, quite flexible in childhood, determine to some degree the basic shape of our physical structure. If those muscles assume a particular tension pattern for any length of time, they can become fixed, affecting later physical growth. What causes the muscles to contract into specific patterns? Very often it is trauma, both physical and mental. If I experience humiliating defeat, my body may assume a physical posture that reflects my feelings. My shoulders will slump, my pelvis will swing forward and tuck under. My arms will hang lifelessly. If I am defeated often enough, that pattern may be imprinted in the clay. And over the years, my body will tell its own history without a word from me. A person who is repeatedly disappointed looks that way. You can see it in the face, posture, and general attitude.

Denise: A Disappointed Body

To see the experience of disappointment in the body, let us consider the case of Denise, a computer analyst living in Los Angeles who has been conducting a long-distance relationship with Tony, a man she met while on a business trip to Chicago. At their first meeting, Tony informed her that his company planned to transfer him to California within the year. On the strength of this possibility, Denise had allowed herself greater involvement in the relationship. But she now reads an E-mail from Tony in which he reports that his company has decided to keep him in the Midwest. Deeply disappointed, Denise moves through the six-stage process.

Initially she reacts with alarm. Her body stiffens, and her face registers surprise. Her eyebrows rise, her eyes open wide; the upper eyelids raise, the lower relax. Her jaw drops, and her mouth opens slightly. These reactions are fleeting and momentary. They are quickly replaced by feelings of frustration and anger. Resistance to accepting the new state of affairs appears on her face. Her eyebrows are now drawn down and together. Her eyes become hard and penetrating. They have a narrow focus and the lower eyelids are tense. Her mouth is closed firmly, lips pressing against each other.

Her body appears energized by protest. Her shoulders, upper back, and arms seem ready to move. Then, just as suddenly, these reactions are replaced by the dominant physical characteristic of disappointment: deflation. Think of a balloon filled to capacity with air. You have only to gently touch it and it bounces off your hand and into the atmosphere. Now imagine the same balloon without air. It is soft and lifeless. You hold it and it sags ingloriously in your hand. All elasticity is gone. This is analogous to what happens to the body during the fifth stage of the disappointment process. It diminishes in size, reflecting the experienced loss and dispossession.

Observing Denise, we notice her shoulders drop and slump. Her head moves forward slightly. Her torso loses its upright quality and seems to collapse into itself. Her arms hang loosely at her sides. There is no vitality in her hands. Her breathing becomes shallow and her eyes look tired and downward. The inner corners of her upper eyelids are pulled up in sadness while the lower eyelids are raised slightly. There is less muscle tone in her face and throughout her entire body. She looks passive and drained — a disappointed woman.

Denise's physical reaction to disappointment is marked by three fundamental characteristics: deflation, energy loss, and restricted breathing. In recalling their disappointments, many of the patients I have treated comment specifically on these physical changes. Barbara, a lively thirty-year-old psychology graduate student, reported: "After my husband broke his ankle and our first vacation in two years was canceled, I felt pretty awful. I had really needed to get away. I remember going shopping to try to lift my spirits. But each time I tried on something and saw myself in the three-way mirror, I felt worse. I looked terrible. My body appeared just as I felt, collapsed and defeated. I felt like I had just run a marathon, except I wasn't even sweating. I had no idea I was so disappointed until the sight of myself in that mirror clued me into the obvious."

And Janet, a successful real estate developer, complained after she had failed to close a deal: "I was so disappointed I could barely lug my body around. I felt like a dead weight. It was an effort to stand up straight. I thought to myself, why bother?"

This is the transitory, physical experience of simple disappointment. Even if the picture is obscured by the intentional inhibition of bodily expression, the characteristics of deflation, energy loss, and restricted breathing are recognizable in muted and evanescent form. But what happens when disappointment is a habitual condition? What is observable in the body of the chronically disappointed individual?

The Posture of Defeat

Take a moment to stand in a comfortable upright position. Close your eyes and consider what mood or condition your stance expresses. Does it seem defiant, removed, aggressive? Perhaps it is so familiar its meaning escapes you. If so, look in a mirror and exaggerate the postural tendencies until you can extract their significance. Now lock your knees, pull in your abdomen, square your shoulders, and puff out your chest. Hold your head erect and tuck in your chin. What state does this posture express? How different is it from your normal position? Notice that the simple act of standing in a particular manner influences your mood. The suggested military posture evokes feelings of invulnerability. The tension pattern underlying the stance gives you a sense of being armored, untouchable, and invincible. There is a noticeable absence of "soft" feeling.

Posture not only expresses feeling, it evokes it. Physical sensations influence what we feel. The mood expressed by a particular standing pattern is self-perpetuating. Posture responds to feeling, which in turn responds to posture. We tend to lock into one way of being upright because, once we are in it, the pattern reinforces itself.

We know that the primary physical experience associated with disappointment is deflation. Consider how a deflated stance would appear. The head droops forward out of line with the torso. The shoulders are rounded and pulled forward. The chest is deflated and falls into itself at the sternum. The abdomen collapses in the umbilicus region, creating the appearance of being foreshortened. There is a forward tilt to the pelvis, which is tucked under in the beaten fashion of a dog with its tail between its legs. The arms hang without vitality. The mood of the posture suggests defeat. The individual looks as if there is no future, only the constant repetition of past emotional losses. Think of a Picasso portrait from his Blue Period, or the melancholy strains of a Chopin nocturne. An individual who habitually stands in this manner will feel the hopelessness suggested by the position.

A basic and critical assumption of body analysis is that your relationship to the ground — how you stand on your own two feet — correlates with how you deal with the practical realities of life. If you're "out of balance," "up in the air," "heavy-footed," and so forth, you are "ungrounded." This means simply that you are standing in a way that prevents adequate contact with the ground. Your physical connection with the floor or earth is impaired in some manner. Like posture, groundedness shares a reciprocal relationship with psychological character. Those who stand rigidly or tentatively are psychologically ungrounded as well. Their link to basic needs, feelings, and sensations is disturbed. Unsupported by their legs, they are also poorly rooted in their relationship to their body. This lack of connection either produces overintellectualized responses or impulsive, sometimes hysterical behaviors. Both are self-defeating and lead to high levels of anxiety and frustration. Ungrounded individuals do not see reality clearly. They depend on illusion to avoid recognition of their dysfunctional patterns.

One might predict that the habitually disappointed would be ungrounded. After all, their expectations for life are most often unrealistic and impossible to satisfy. In fact, chronically disappointed individuals often stand with their knees and ankles held rigidly, as if they were locked. The lower halves of their bodies may appear stiff and tense, without grace and strength. The legs may look a bit like stilts. There is no flexibility or ease of movement. The general impression is that they are bracing themselves against falling. This image is most descriptive. Because habitually disappointed individuals have been let down time and again, they stand rigidly as a defense against the inevitable fall into disillusionment. As long as their assessment of possibility is faulty, their stance upon the earth will reflect their insecurity and lack of rootedness.

The Despairing Face

The face is the most expressive part of the human body; it is also the easiest to mask. It may reflect our deepest feelings or appear as inscrutable as the classic psychoanalyst. It is capable of portraying a life story or simply the emotion of the moment. Mobile, changeable, complex, it is the principal means by which we identify ourselves and recognize others. Yet we rarely observe the detail of each other's faces. In conversation we may look at our friends, but only to the extent required to read their expression and react accordingly. We perceive agreement, hostility, boredom, and so forth, but we infrequently observe the character of the face. Like looking at a clock and noting only that you are not late without registering the actual time, we observe faces from a practical point of view. We extract what we need to know. The rest we ignore. Of course, there are exceptions to this practice; lovers gazing intently at each other, mothers observing their newborn children, artists scrutinizing their models. If I asked you to describe in detail the features of a friend's face would you be up to the task?

The face of the chronically disappointed person shows defeat and sadness. Signs of these feelings can be read in the eyes, forehead, mouth, and overall expression. None of the anger and protestation which we noticed in Denise's face is apparent. After so much accumulated disappointment, there is less resistance to conceding what has come to be regarded as a common experience. The disappointed face is drawn and tired. The muscle tone may be poor with noticeable deadness — a lack of energy — around the cheekbones. There is no brightness or gleam in the eyes, but instead the bleak quality associated with hopelessness. The mouth is tightly held, unable to risk reaching out and suffering another disappointment. Its corners are turned down in sorrow. The jaw is sometimes set in a fixed position, as if to hold back the need to cry. The forehead may be troubled and wrinkled, expressing a quality of world-weariness. The disappointed face reminds me of a visage from childhood: the unhappy clown whose countenance provides us with a caricature of disappointment that is simultaneously moving and disturbing.

Breathing: Sigh without Relief

The simple act of breathing is both commonplace and miraculous. You take thousands of breaths each day, with little awareness of the process, leaving it all up to the regulation of the hypothalamus and medulla oblongata. They must be doing an adequate job or you wouldn't be reading this book right now! Breathing is an involuntary, generally unconscious process that is also subject to volitional control. You can change your breathing pattern — the rate and cadence — by intention. You can hold your breath for some length of time, or you can pant rapidly. Many variations are possible. When you inhale oxygen into your lungs, the diaphragm — a thin, muscular, tendinous sheath which separates the abdomen from the heart and lungs — descends to allow for expansion of the rib cage. At the same time the spinal column elongates and rocks the pelvis forward. During exhalation the opposite movement occurs, with the diaphragm ascending and pushing air out of the lungs. Full respiration creates a wavelike motion throughout the torso.

There is a direct relationship between breathing patterns and the intensity of feelings. When breathing is superficial and the diaphragm and muscles around the rib cage are tense, we humans experience less sensation and emotion. We feel cut off from part of ourselves. Full respiration creates the opposite situation. Our bodies are replenished with oxygen. We are sensitive to sensation and feel energetic, alive, and mobile.

Breathing patterns have a tendency to become fixed over time, but they are frequently modified by immediate experience. A terrifying movie will cause most members of the audience to hold their breath, thereby restricting oxygen intake. A quick sprint to get out of the rain will charge the body with oxygen and may release tension in the diaphragm. Similarly, the experience of disappointment has its own effects on breathing. The chronically disappointed individual shows constricted respiration. His diaphragm does not move easily, and he may have some difficulty inhaling. This condition reflects the generally dismayed and resigned attitude that accompanies disappointment: It's just not worth the effort. Full respiration is an assertion of one's right to exist. It is a statement of vitality and security. Disappointed individuals are too defeated to accomplish such an action, nor would they want to. Breathing fully would bring them into contact with their dissatisfaction. Limited respiration helps them to restrict the degree of feeling they experience.

On the biological level, disappointed individuals are caught in the expiration phase of the breath cycle. It is as if they are stuck in a brief but repeated sigh. Inspiration then becomes taxing because the deep-seated tension in the muscles between the ribs hold the chest in a deflated position. The defeat associated with disappointment creates a restricted breathing style that reinforces itself. But like posture, these self-perpetuating patterns can be changed through awareness and intention. As Kazantzakis reminded us in *Zorba the Greek:* "As I now knew the name of my affliction, I could perhaps conquer it more easily. It was no longer elusive and incorporeal; it had assumed a name and a shape, and it would be easier for me to combat it...."

Chapter 4

Life Cycle Disappointments

To grow older is a new venture in itself.
— Goethe

When my friends and I were studying developmental psychology in graduate school, we used to tell the following anecdote:

A middle aged man is so worried about losing his hair that he feels depressed and anxious most of the time. His appetite falls off, and he has difficulty getting to sleep at night. In desperation he seeks professional help.

His physician takes one look at him and decides he is too run down. For his own good, he needs to reduce the stress level in his life. The doctor recommends a long vacation in the Bahamas, a job change, and a bottle of Prozac.

Unsatisfied, the man visits a psychoanalyst, who concludes that he's suffering from unresolved Oedipal feelings reawakened by his wife's interest in a new career. He advises a four-year course of analysis, with sessions three times a week.

Feeling worse than ever, the man confesses his problems to his hair stylist. "Don't sweat it," she says, "just wear a hat."

As we move through the life cycle, we must contend with the struggles inherent in each of the different phases. These "crises" of development are sometimes mistaken for signs of deeper and more profound problems. Our balding friend is suffering only from the adult growth pains inherent in the midlife passage. Recognizing these developmental stages enables individuals to move through them with less angst.

Not surprisingly, it was Freud who offered the first systematic theory of human development. He emphasized that the important psychosexual periods of growth were centered exclusively in childhood. His five stages — oral, anal, phallic, latent, and genital — continue to be debated today.

Developmental psychology offers a contrasting perspective: that the individual changes throughout the entire lifespan from conception to death. Adulthood is not a personally stagnant period of fifty years, but a succession of life phases, each with its own specific challenges. Indeed, the entire process of maturation requires struggling against the counterforces of stagnation.

With the exception of Gail Sheehy's widely read book *Passages*, which popularized this perspective a decade ago, developmental psychology has rarely been in the public eye. Yet over the years it has become a powerful intellectual force, encompassing a diverse body of knowledge, from the theories of mental evolution propounded by pioneer psychologist G. Stanley Hall to the "constructionism" of Swiss researcher Jean Piaget.

The writings of Erik Erikson have particularly influenced the developmental point of view. In his seminal work *Childhood and Society*, Erikson set forth eight life stages, each containing a "psychosocial" crisis in which two conflicting tendencies within the individual are reconciled. Adolescence, for example, is seen as a period in which young people struggle to define themselves. It is the confrontation between the inclination to develop identity and the concern with how one is seen by others that characterizes this phase and gives it a tumultuous quality.

Erikson's basic assumptions are helpful in understanding our own changes. They can be summarized in this way:

- Human development reveals itself through symptoms of apparent discord; yet it is this struggle between opposite tendencies that produces maturity.

- The process of change is continuous throughout life and does not cease once adulthood is reached.

- Individuals move through growth stages when they are ready, not according to a strict chronological timetable. For some people the issues faced during middle age may come a decade later than for others.

Developmental Disappointments

The stages of the life cycle are characterized not only by the struggle of conflicting tendencies but also by the appearance of disappointments specific to a particular period of life. Since each new stage of life demands that we surrender some of the comfortable behavior and attitude patterns of the previous stage, there is always a feeling of loss and disappointment accompanying each change. Expectations of adolescence don't fit easily into young adulthood, and so on up the developmental ladder. Thus the thirteen-year-old, although eager to assume adult privilege, is sorely disappointed when forced to relinquish the special protective relationship with parents.

Beyond this point, however, there are disappointments built into the process of acquiring worldliness. As we age, more of our dreams and wishes are challenged by the accumulation of life experience. At thirty-five it is harder than it was at sixteen to hold onto the illusion that justice governs human relations. At sixty-five, such a wish is already dead and buried. The loss of these illusions produces a sense of disappointment as what we expect from life is constantly undermined by the tough lessons of experience.

In the rest of this chapter, we'll take a look at the inherent disappointments within six life passages: infancy/childhood, adolescence, young adulthood, early middle age, middle age, and later adulthood.

Infancy/Childhood

From the moment of conception through preadolescence, the child shows unequaled growth — intellectually, emotionally, and physically. If everything proceeds smoothly — and this is a big "if" — the young organism will acquire before puberty a basic sense of trust, self-control, independence, purpose, and competence. This is not an easy period of development. Beginning in the first months of life, the infant is caught in a dilemma between the desire for continued and repeated gratification and an equally relentless demand by the parents to behave in a socially acceptable manner (the conflict between instinct and culture). In struggling to find some resolution, the child uses fantasy as a means of providing security. Wishes allow a measure of imagined control over circumstance. And in the child's view of things, wishes and expectations are virtually the same thing.

Disappointment flourishes in childhood for just this reason. Because the child's expectations are colored by fantasy without the counterbalance of life experience, they are poorly conceived and frequently go unmet. The failure of an expectation is felt as a tangible loss by the young, who have no sense of perspective and endow their wishes with symbolic meaning. This is why the smallest frustration may evoke as grand a reaction as a major loss.

The vast world of illusion which we encourage in children through "Disneyesque" or synthetic folk tales, myths, and stories also creates the preconditions for disappointment. We teach children to believe in miracles, happy endings, gratification of true desire, good and evil, Santa Claus. These ideas, which represent our own deeper wishes for a sweeter and more benign reality, are used to maintain and nurture the innocence of the young. In their own way they provide the child with reassurance against imagined fears and pain. The developing ego is not yet ready to face the true nature of the world. Reality must be accepted gradually, paced to the individual's growing internal strength.

The problem, of course, is that in protecting the fragile burgeoning self, we cause other problems. When the five-year-old discovers there's no such thing as Santa Claus, she feels let down and shaken, and wonders what else is not true. Still, such disappointments rarely scar. There's a resiliency in childhood that enables the young to tolerate most disillusioning experience without unfavorable consequence. Beside the usual disappointments with which every parent is familiar, there are four unavoidable and developmentally linked experiences that do have a major impact on the child. These involve restrictions on gratification, incest, and Oedipal desires. The impact occurs when the child discovers that:

- Gratification is not always available. You can't always get what you want when you want it.

- Gratification is highly conditional. You must behave in a certain manner to get what you desire. Sometimes even the "correct" behavior doesn't produce the wished-for outcome.

- An exclusive physical and emotional relationship with the mother is prohibited.

- An exclusive relationship with the opposite-sex parent, shutting out the same-sex parent, is prohibited.

Adolescence

Extended in Western society by the delay of marriage and the requirements of higher education, the period of adolescence contains both the heady fragrance of freedom and the moldy odors of childhood dependence. It is a transitional period with its own values, lifestyle, and peer pressures, but it often appears as a way of life unto itself. Few of us would choose to relive our adolescence. Indeed, we want to *forget* the humiliations and cruelties suffered through youthful ignorance and exuberance. Struggling to develop a sense of independent identity, yet still requiring the emotional support provided by the family, adolescents are caught in a bind. They have an incessant and powerful urge to be free, but they lack the ability and maturity to handle full responsibility.

This is a chaotic time in the life of the individual. Young people must contend with innumerable pressures. For one thing, their bodies are changing rapidly and these changes create all sorts of doubt and confusion. "Who am I?" is no longer a psychological question, but a physical one as well. In response, teenagers experiment by "trying on" various roles and appearances. They may dress and behave conventionally one day, bizarrely and newly pierced the next. Or they may act promiscuously, wear seductive clothes and an overabundance of makeup. Such experiments are indirect attempts at addressing the troubling and persistent issue of identity.

Disappointments in adolescence are varied, encompassing the general areas of concern in this period: peer-group acceptance, biological changes, restrictions on initiative and choice. Underlying all these difficulties is the uneasy issue of selfhood.

Peer-group disappointments revolve around failure to be recognized as desirable, conforming, and, therefore, worthwhile. These are the typical teenage disappointments portrayed in the popular media. Exclusion from the "in" group, unrequited love, and the disloyalty of friends receive a great deal of attention because the issues of popularity and worth are closely connected. Teenagers, uncertain of themselves, often interpret rejection experiences as indications of their value.

Disappointment with one's newly-emerging physical self may be unspoken, but anyone who remembers adolescence knows the importance of this issue. Anxiety about height, weight, breast size, genital development, and facial characteristics is heightened. Rapid growth, which produces physical and psychological awkwardness, sometimes misconstrued as permanent, creates additional doubts. Comparison of one's physical attributes with those of an idealized favorite also increases the level of disappointment.

To the ten-year-old who mimics his older brother or simply observes the externals of adolescent life, the period seems ideal. I have rarely talked with a young person who was not looking forward to the teenage years, with their appearance of freedom, self-regulation, and excitement. When the ten-year-old grows up, however, he discovers that the free and easy attitude is only one part of the story. Life isn't as much fun as it appeared to be. There are pressures from school, peer group, and parents. Freedom is conditional and frequently restricted; responsibilities increase and, with them, disappointment.

Although the adolescent looks like an adult, he or she is very much a youth in the eyes of those in authority. This situation is, perhaps, the greatest disappointment of the period. It leads to a feeling of being misunderstood — a theme which permeates the songs and myths of the subculture. To the teenager, restrictions on freedom are an arbitrary affront to a growing sense of adulthood. To the parents, they are a recognition that their offspring are not mature enough to handle the responsibility of self-regulation. The battle between restricting adult and freedom-craving adolescent goes on in every generation. The result is a continual series of disappointments rooted in a false expectation of unlimited freedom and privilege.

Young Adulthood (Twenty to Thirty-two years)

The early part of this life phase is filled with promise, aspiration, and possibility. Consequently, it is heavily weighted with anxiety and relatively free of disappointment. No longer shackled by the restrictions of childhood and the ambiguity of adolescence, young adults are in search of a direction and purpose, a mentor or guide, and a relationship that can deepen and provide security. This is a time when the focus on "me" is broadened to an emphasis on "we," when isolation and loneliness are replaced by community and friendship, and when participation in society brings satisfaction. Freud was once asked what distinguishes the healthy from the neurotic personality. He replied that it is the ability to love and to work. These are precisely the struggles of this period in the life cycle — to build relationships and to find a suitable occupation.

In *Passages*, Gail Sheehy suggests two other urges in this stage: to build firm, safe structures for the future, and to explore and experiment, keeping all things tentative. The relationship between these opposing inclinations gives the phase its particular character, and reveals something about the specific needs of the individual who follows either extreme.

Young adulthood is still a time of unchallenged illusion. There is as yet not enough life experience to dampen one's expectation of an "anything's possible" tomorrow. The adult role is too new and probationary, too prejudiced by the nervousness of first experience to allow for the farsighted perspective that comes with age. Particular illusions carried from childhood begin to surface in this phase. Sheehy points out three:

- Willpower overcomes all.

- There is one true course in life.

- I'm unique.

To the young person putting down first roots in an adult world, not many things are certain. Jobs may come and go, money is in short supply, love appears and floats away on the evening breeze. But through it all, one idea is sustaining: *I will — by virtue of my desire — persevere. My will can conquer adversity.* This is a typical attitude of the early and middle twenties and may be the only thing unequivocal in a time of general uncertainty. Hand in hand with this belief goes another less confident proposition: *There is one true course in life and I must find it.* Indeed, this is the task of the young adult who is faced with so many "first" choices in the twenties. The idea that there may be countless roads from A to B is usually rejected because of its ambiguity and the cultural pressure to find a personal direction.

The attempt to create certainty where there is none explains why young people are susceptible to the irrefutability of gurus or the demand of *shoulds:* "I should live a life of social significance." "I should get proper training while I'm still young." And so forth. Individuals in this period are also convinced that they have arrived at their choices through a process purely of their own making. In

defining themselves through their actions, they rarely see that
their preferences may be a reaction to their family of origin, or
that they are based on internalized family values or societal
injunctions. They view their decisions as uncontaminated, a
helpful distortion that leads to feelings of uniqueness and positive
self-esteem.

Disappointment, especially during the early part of this stage,
is less common. Great expectations remain as yet untested. If
disappointments are experienced, they are generally cast aside
quickly. There is so much future that the loss of one or two
possibilities is trivial. This is a time of expansiveness; anxiety about
the road ahead is counterbalanced by the loftiness of one's own
illusions. Doubts are hidden beneath resolve. Somehow a happy
ending is seen as inevitable despite surrounding evidence to the
contrary.

In the latter part of this phase, however, disappointment
comes knocking, particularly disillusionment in self. By the late
twenties and early thirties, the wide-open promise of an
unparalleled future starts to fade and the first extended look at self
is honestly taken. Up until this point, confrontations with identity
have been secretive glances colored by hopeful deception. But the
repetitive patterns of behavior and feelings are now too noticeable
to avoid, and the protective environments of home and school no
longer obstruct young people from taking a long hard look at
themselves. A protective veil has been lifted after the incubation
of childhood and adolescence.

Paula, a thirty-one-year-old journalist and editor for a weekly
county newspaper, spoke about this experience in her life:

> *It's hard for me to admit just how little I knew about myself
> until a few years ago. I thought I was a pretty healthy person
> with no real psychological problems and a positive outlook
> on life. I considered my family to be rather normal, no*

hangups worth mentioning. No problems with Mom, just an occasional disagreement. I thought my sisters felt the same way, although we rarely talked about the family.

Then, a few years ago, I started to realize I was having problems with my close relationships. I used to blame it on the men I dated. This guy wasn't trustworthy, so I couldn't get close to him. That one had problems with commitment. Another reminded me too much of Dad. After this went on for a while, I began to see that even though these men were not right for me, it was I who was choosing them. I knew they were afraid of getting close, but maybe I was too. That's probably why I chose them in the first place —so I wouldn't have to commit myself.

I began talking to my sisters about this and about our family. I realized how much I'd forgotten about what happened in our home. We all agreed it wasn't a bed of roses. It certainly wasn't the happy time I pretended it was. I feel sad about that. It wasn't the way I wanted it to be.

Surrendering her self-protective myths and feelings, Paula recognized that fear of commitment was a pattern in her life. Everyone maintains some necessary self-fiction, but by the early thirties most individuals have had enough life experience to recognize neurotic sexual attitudes, self-defeating and self-deprecating behaviors, poor relationship choices, and work-related difficulties. With eyes opened to these patterns, frustration and disappointment starts to show up, and typically many people begin psychotherapy. Ironically, it is the acknowledgment of disappointment in ourselves that helps us to make the personal changes necessary for a healthy transition to middle adulthood.

Unfortunately, the depth of our disillusionment is just beginning to be known. The notorious "midlife crisis" is about to ensnare us and shake our very foundations.

Early Middle Age (Thirty-three to Forty-five years)

I first met Peter at a party ten years ago, just after he had finished his residency in internal medicine. Ironically, we spoke then about the great prospects that awaited us as we both embarked on new careers. Peter had followed the life script that had been laid out for him many years before. He had always worked hard, gotten top grades, gone to the best schools, and achieved whatever goals he had set out for himself. A successful medical career was the next challenge.

Just after college, Peter married a woman with a similar middle-class background. While he was in medical school, Chris assumed the role of breadwinner. But as with so many student marriages, the stress of long hours of study, the time apart, and the different worlds in which they lived took their toll. They began to fight continually. Positive feelings of love and affection were buried under long, exhausting arguments. They debated everything, from politics to the value of certain kitchen appliances. When Peter graduated from medical school, the marriage broke up.

For over a year, the effects of all that struggling weighed heavily on him. He was bitter. Misogyny leaked out from the reservoir of hurt and resentment. Gradually, he reconstituted himself and, focusing on work, got on with his life. A few years later he married another woman, very different from his first wife. Elaine was the physical opposite — tall and blond — with a vastly different personal history.

Peter's career as a physician went along without a hitch. He was successful, as he had been at most things in the past. He and

Elaine had two children. They bought a large house with a sunny backyard, plenty of room for a garden, a large swing, and a tree house. They had no financial problems. Peter's practice nearly doubled within two years, and Elaine worked as a telecommunications consultant.

During this time, he seemed to settle into his life. He joined a number of local organizations, took responsibility for the garden and landscaping around the house, spent time with his children, and worked long hours teaching and treating patients at one of the local hospitals. To the outside observer, his was a life to envy. No major problems. No economic worries. A good marriage.

Peter could not tell you precisely why, but in his late thirties he began to lose interest in his relationship with his wife. They rarely fought, as he had done so often in his first marriage, and they shared mutual interests. The only thing Peter could say with certainty was that there was no passion between them. Perhaps there never was, but he was now very aware of it and he felt bored. The relationship was too predictable. He knew her opinions before she expressed them. He knew what she would wear, what words she would use to describe an experience. He felt he understood too much about Elaine; the mystery of their differences had died.

When he reached his early forties, the feelings of ennui which he had tried to ignore began to spread to other parts of his life. He was bored with the same routines at work, the same faces and tasks. He was tired of getting into his car each morning and driving identical roads to the same destination. He was uninterested in his conventional friends and their colorless conversation:

> *Everything I do feels as if I've done it before, and not just once or twice but hundreds of times. My life is a permanent deja vu. There's no excitement, except for my kids and the thought of escaping to some exotic paradise. I thought there*

*was more to life than this. I believed that if I worked hard
I would be rewarded and those rewards would keep me
going. Well, I've gotten what I wanted but it doesn't interest
me anymore. None of it matters. "What was all that effort
for?"*

The midlife impasse of the middle thirties and early forties is
as predictable as the politician's election year promise. If the last
half of young adulthood is a time of disappointment in self, then
this is a period of disappointment in life.

According to Erik Erikson, the challenge of the mid-adult
phase is to create a synthesis, pulling together all aspects of one's
life into a meaningful whole. Productivity and creativity combine
with feelings for others and culminate in the development of
"generativity" — concern for guiding the next generation. When
this characteristic fails to evolve, the individual stagnates,
pseudointimacy develops, and there is a sense of personal
impoverishment. The midlife crisis reflects the struggle to
establish meaning in one's existence and prevent stagnation and
world weariness.

As we move steadily into middle age, several things converge.
We settle into a "long-term" lifestyle that has an appearance of
permanence. Up until now, there have been regular and frequent
adaptive changes demanded by life's exigencies. The structure of
the educational system, for example, created a major upheaval
every four years or so from high school to postgraduate or
professional training. Then too, there were other urgent matters:
the jockeying for the right job, the search for the compatible life
partner, the purchase of the new house, the birth of the first child.
By the mid-thirties most of the natural "beginnings" in life have
been encountered and a measure of stability is introduced. We
have found a course to follow and have committed ourselves to it.
The period of preparation is over. It is time to live.

With this settling-in experience comes our first extended contact with repetition and monotony. Each day looks very much like the last. Rituals and patterns become firmly established. Constancy produces security, but it also creates tedium. Even arenas of challenge and excitement like work and sex can become prisons of redundancy.

Repetition in early middle age produces a sense of emptiness. We get restless. We feel trapped. We notice with regret that the fervor of our youth is gone. With surprise we recognize our corruptibility for the first time. We begin to use the word "jaded" in describing ourselves.

This is also a period when we encounter the initial signs of our mortality. As we move beyond the halfway point, the symbolic significance of this chronological juncture is not lost on us. There's not that much time left. We notice as well that physical beauty and endurance begins to fade. Our faces show the strain of too little sleep and too much anxiety. The character lines are firmly and obviously etched. The wrinkles encountered each morning are permanent fixtures in the flesh. Our bodies also display signs of sagging. Tissue accumulates in the wrong places. Bulges no longer disappear with moderate dieting. The recuperation rate from misuse and overindulgence lengthens dramatically. The pulled muscle takes longer to heal and longer to relax. All these indications are concrete evidence that physical being is finite. Our bodies will not go on forever. Will is no match for time.

Beyond these facts, we are also faced with the realization that our alternatives are shrinking. As youths, we had numerous paths to take and seemingly all the time in the world to take them. Now we are saddled with responsibilities, tangible physical limitations, and fewer years in which to accomplish anything. Our options are reduced geometrically by these considerations. The naive, world-embracing optimism of the adolescent, which could declare without self-consciousness, "I'm going to be president of a multi-national corporation, raise children, and help the homeless!" has been reduced to a more modest level, in keeping with midlife realities.

Taken together, all these factors — repetition, ennui, mortality, shrinking possibility — produce severe disillusionment with life. Indeed, this is a period of great disappointment that often leads to depression. Some individuals experiment with sexual promiscuity, imbibe large quantities of alcohol and drugs, or throw all caution to the wind and flirt openly with death (parachuting, car-racing) to escape the distress. Generally, such attempts create other problems of even greater severity.

The disappointments of midlife revolve around one central theme which will be repeated once more at life's finale: "Now that I know what it's really about, I'm disappointed that that's all there is." The other disappointments of this period in love, work, family, level of accomplishment, and loss of beauty and youth are merely variations on this theme. Midlife disenchantment is essentially a crisis of disillusionment. We have lived over 50 percent of our allotted time only to find that the illusions we have treasured since childhood have all been maimed or destroyed by uncompromising reality. We plaintively ask, "Is that all there is?" because what we have experienced doesn't measure up to what we expected, what we imagined, and what we wished life would be.

The mid-adult passage is a period in which we redefine our expectations, substituting a wiser, more tolerant and accepting perspective for the romantic and illusory hopes of youth. Those who make it successfully through this phase have engineered such an adaptation. Perhaps they have changed careers, developed new interests, encouraged their creative selves to flourish. What is important is that they have established authentic goals for themselves — independent of the programmed expectations of their childhood and society — and that their new direction is rooted in a mature knowledge of possibility. Even more significant, however, is that they have learned to appreciate what they have and to find joy in the small and fleeting moments of beauty, tenderness, and laughter that life provides. Ultimately, the key to a successful midlife transition is in developing the capacity to feel gratitude, especially for life itself. (More on this in Chapter 11.)

Middle Age (Forty-five to Sixty-four years)

This time of life has been considered only recently as a separate period by developmental psychologists. With the gradual increase in life expectancy and the new cultural concern for the aging process, it has emerged as a critical phase in the life cycle, with its particular satisfactions and its characteristic problems and disappointments. "On the wrong side of forty," but far from dotage, individuals have by this point developed a repertoire of behaviors to cope with most life challenges. Indeed, according to both popular myth and established fact, it is men in this age group who control most of the nation's wealth and run the country, determining our collective future in the cloak and board rooms nationwide.

In terms of money and privilege, middle age is the prime of life — a time when power and ability are at their peak. Income is at its highest level and the percentage of families below the subsistence level is well under the national average. Likewise, the number of families living in homes they own is higher than in any other age grouping.

With the midlife crisis safely behind, this stage is distinguished by renewed steadiness and permanence. Mobility decreases. Roots grow deeper. Life patterns become entrenched. Between 1975 and

1980, only twenty-seven percent of those in this life phase moved their primary residence. This figure represents half the rate of those under forty-five years of age. Although on the rise, the number of divorces is also less than the national average. After years of being coupled, the motivation to live alone or to start again in a new relationship drops off. Clearly, these are years in which one settles into a stable and patterned existence without disruptive changes.

But these are by no means problem-free years. In fact, depression, alcoholism, and suicide are major concerns in the middle-age population. The death of one's spouse, the empty-nest syndrome, the fears associated with retirement, menopausal problems, and the changing roles of women are but a few of the difficulties encountered during this time.

Ruth's story illustrates the economic disappointments that may characterize this period. A fifty-three-year-old high school teacher with a husband and three children, Ruth was a working mother all her adult life. She played the unheralded role of "superwoman," getting her family off to work and school each morning, cooking meals, and keeping the house, while at the same time contending with an often frustrating full-time job:

> *How did I do it? I didn't think about it. I worked because I wanted to and we needed the money. But I also wanted a family so I raised my kids the best I could, which was pretty darn good considering the circumstances. When you want something enough you find a way to get it. That's all!*

With the children grown up and away on their own, however, Ruth's life did not go as expected. Her husband suffers from heart disease and she has tired of teaching in the racially torn school system in which she has worked for over twenty-five years.

I thought that when I reached fifty, my life would get easier. The problem of juggling two careers would be solved when my kids left home. I expected that Sol and I would be pretty comfortable financially, and so on. But with Sol's illness, we don't have the money for a leisurely way of life. I'm still working too hard and getting too little back for a woman of my age. At this point, I had hoped to enjoy a little more comfort.

In later middle age, we expect to reap the harvest of our labor. We want an easing of career pressures and the stresses of raising a family. We hope to put our lives on automatic pilot some of the time and live more comfortably with greater affluence. It's a time when we say to ourselves, "If I don't enjoy my life now, I never will!" Yet with two people working in 80 percent of American families, Social Security threatened, and the death of job security, baby boomer expectations are uncertain. As Ruth says, "I can't keep going like I did before. Even spring chickens get old. When you're at my stage of life, you don't want to slow down — you *need* to."

Other disappointments during this phase: At work, younger employees may be getting the promotions. The fifty-year-old executive is vulnerable to career plateau and has to contend with the possibility of stalled advancement. At home, the parent struggling to balance children and career finds her kids have flown the coop and she has to readjust to the loss of her maternal role. Changes wrought by the information and technology revolution may cause people to look at the surrounding landscape and long for the accustomed conventions and lifestyles of the past. "Why can't the world be more like it used to be?" is a familiar lament. It reflects disappointment in the current state of affairs. The longing for the familiarity of the "good ol' days" seems to increase with age.

Later Adulthood (Sixty-five years and over)

We are a nation obsessed with youth, fearful of death, and either indifferent or callous in our attitude toward older citizens. It is only in recent years that we have begun to address the varied problems of the elderly. Many of these have social origins. In Japan, a country in which the nuclear family remains relatively intact and the aged are revered and sought out for their wisdom, the difficulties associated with the last years of life are largely absent. The devaluation of America's senior population presents not only a moral dilemma but a practical one as well. A precious natural resource is squandered by our failure to utilize the skills and experience of what T. S. Eliot called our "quiet-voiced elders."

Later adulthood is a period in which the individual wrestles with the issues of integrity and despair. Social attitudes affect this struggle. Will the remainder of life be lived with acceptance of what has transpired and what is fatefully to come, or will it be lived with regret, sadness, and despondency? Will the individual accept "one's one-and-only life cycle as something that had to be and that, by necessity, permitted of no substitutions," as Erikson puts it, or will that person sink into remorse and cynicism, both symptoms of a fear of death?

The elderly must contend with aloneness, the dwindling of physical abilities, illness, the death of friends, and, most importantly, the loss of hope, for the final act contains no encores. Life has run its course. There will be no more surprises. It will never get better. Individuals who concede these realities and still maintain an appreciation of their individual journey, an acceptance of the limits of life, its celebrations and disappointments, and a recognition of its wonder do not fear death.

They acknowledge it as the final stage of living.

The disappointments of old age are all connected to an unwillingness to accept death. In one way or another they are statements decrying the loss of future. Here are three to consider:

- I will not be remembered.

- I haven't done all that I wanted!

- Is that all there is?

The failure to leave one's mark on the world — to be forgotten — is the oldest of fears. It is based not only on a desire to maintain some measure of immortality, but on the belief that one's life cannot have had significance if it failed to make an impact on the world. Similarly, frustration over one's level of accomplishment is related to a dread of personal inconsequence. This concern is fed by present circumstance, for the elderly doubt their ability to contribute to contemporary life.

These disappointments protest the failure of particular expectations for meaning and significance, but more than this, they bemoan the end of expecting itself. For many, the infamous question, "is that all there is?" is a bit like the one-liner, "The food is terrible, and such small portions!" Regardless of its drawbacks, we want more of life, another chance to make it meet our expectations.

From the vantage point of old age looking back at the roads not taken, the opportunities missed, the failures of nerve, the chance losses, it is easy to focus on what might have been and to live with regret. The danger of this passage is that we will be overwhelmed with the unfairness, difficulties, and pain of existence; that we will bemoan our fate and howl to the gods as we selectively remember the events of our personal histories. Bitterness and disappointment fill the halls of nursing homes everywhere. It is difficult to find justification and meaning in life.

Even those who have lived within the boundaries of established religion are hard pressed to explain senseless injustice and prejudice.

Yet it is in this later period that the disappointed condition takes on the clarity of a full moon on a pitch-black night. With no second chances, there is little point in holding out for the wishes and expectations that can never be. There is only a single path out of regret: to accept life for what it is and what it has been, regardless of whether it falls short of one's dreams. With this understanding comes relief and joy. It is such a simple idea, yet so difficult to put into practice.

Chapter 5

Socially Induced Disappointments

In America, an hour is fifty minutes.
— German Proverb

They are not men, they are not women, they are Americans.
— Pablo Picasso

A merica was conceived and born on a bed of wishes: for the elimination of a class society, for equal opportunity and justice regardless of race or religion, for tolerance and acceptance of all peoples, for prosperity and abundance for those who work hard. Such were the aspirations and hopes of a new country serving as a beacon to the class-oppressed and blood-stained nations of Europe.

Americans, with their legacy of natural resources, Manifest Destiny, and free industrial expansion, have always believed in the dream of endless possibility. We have been taught to expect more, desire more, imagine more. It is the American Way. Bigger cars, bigger houses, bigger dreams. The sky's the limit! America's hidden purpose has been to prove to the rest of the world that history extends only from yesterday to yesterday. The present and future are boundless. Horatio Alger — the honest, hard-working boy who rose from poverty to riches — epitomized the American myth. Success is promised to anyone who is willing to earn it. And for many these dreams have become a reality. Since 1890, every generation has done better than the one preceding it.

But at what cost? Many social observers, including historian Christopher Lasch, have argued that we live in an era of narcissism distinguished by fear of intimacy, pseudo self-insight, loss of historical time, and self-absorption. Lasch's convincing characterization of American society fits the Boom Generation particularly well. Combine material advantage and the excesses of the child-centered family and you have the soil in which narcissism grows best. Whether the peculiar experiences of this group created the upsurge in self-absorption or simply reflect a response to a larger trend is not clear. Lasch contends that the increase in narcissism represents a realistic way to cope with the tensions and anxieties of modern life. Social critic Hans Morgenthau, on the other hand, asserts its expansion is a response to the failure of religion, science, and nationalism to deal with the universal problem of alienation. Whatever the reason for its rise, there is no doubt of its magnitude, and that the Boom Generation is well suited to the current climate. After all, its credo for more than a decade was "Do your own thing!"

Exaltation of the self. Devotion to the transformation of the body, diet books, exercise classes, personal trainers, plastic surgery, magazines with egoistic titles like *Us* and *Self,* armies of young people plugged into the impenetrable universe of their own headphones — all are indications that the preoccupation with "me" has never been more pervasive. There have been other periods in history when the celebration of self has taken precedence. The Renaissance, for example, was such a time. But never before has "self" been the preeminent value.

Psychology has reflected this new interest with not only the emergence of "self-fulfillment" therapies but also the resurgence of more traditional "ego" approaches with their focus on "object relations" and separation-independence issues. The term "pathological narcissist" is bandied about with the same nonchalance as "conversion hysteria" was in Freud's time. The *Diagnostic and Statistical Manual of Mental Disorders IV*, the official source of psychiatric nomenclature, lists the main characteristics of narcissism as: grandiose sense of self-importance or uniqueness; preoccupation with fantasies of unlimited success, power, brilliance; the need for constant attention and admiration; feelings of entitlement; interpersonal exploitativeness; lack of empathy indicated in the inability to recognize how others feel.

In the case of the Boom Generation, doting parents and high expectations joined with social forces to produce an adult population which expected uninterrupted gratification. As one member, a twenty-nine-year-old social service administrator, facetiously put it, "My mother devoted herself to making me feel I'm #1, and I wouldn't want to disappoint her."

Narcissism as a cultural phenomenon is so commonplace that we scarcely notice it. Like the telephone poles and power lines, it has faded into the background. The American ideal of rugged individualism has mutated into the apotheosis of self. We live in a "me first" society which is marked by a decline of interest in the public sphere and social responsibility. Individuals with narcissistic traits are too engrossed in themselves to make the crossover to another's experience. The other person is merely an audience, an admirer to be used and discarded after the applause has subsided. In some quarters, human relations are seen as purely utilitarian arrangements: "I use you. You use me. Everyone's happy." Succeeding by any means, regardless of consequence to others, is easily justifiable under these rules. "People will fend for themselves" is the rationalization used to excuse ruthlessness. At the same time, narcissists are particularly vulnerable to criticism. Their overevaluation of self does not allow them to perceive any frailty in their own persons, and they often react to emotional injury with surprise, anger, and depression. It is as if the very foundation on which they base their self-esteem has been rocked.

In the broadest sense, narcissistic traits are necessary for survival. The energy to meet biological and social needs is drawn from self-interest. We could not defend ourselves against aggression, struggle to put food on the table, or fight for our inalienable rights without some measure of self-consideration. The problem, of course, is one of degree.

Narcissism and Disappointment: An Eternal Partnership

The price we pay for self-gratification is high. Aside from the loss of human community and the excessive level of personal exploitativeness, we are caught in two other traps. Although we place great value on self-determination, we are as individuals more dependent on the society for our basic needs than ever before. The energy companies, supermarkets, and clothing-store chains provide our essential goods and services. Our destinies are shaped by the larger forces of international trade and political advantage. Self-sufficiency is largely an ideal of the past. We may exalt the importance of personal freedom, yet we are physically more dependent than at any other time in American history.

There is a direct relationship between narcissism and disappointment. Self-absorbed individuals tend to overestimate themselves or anything identified with them, such as their car, job, or children. They function under the simple formula: "What's mine is good; what's yours is less good." From this distortion comes another: They are entitled to special treatment by others. They expect attention, love, validation, privilege, and respect without having to earn them. This attitude carries over into their relationship with life, which they view as owing them something. Consequently, they believe their expectations should be met automatically and they resent any frustration of their desires. In the narcissistic view of things, the world revolves around "me." Gratification is a right.

Of course, when the privileges of fifteenth-century royalty are claimed by large numbers of people in our modern culture, some sparks are bound to fly. Narcissistic expectations are completely ungrounded in reality. We know that when expectation is faulty, the result is chronic disappointment. Such is the case with narcissistic individuals. They are always disillusioned because their expectations for themselves and life are too grand, special, and unique.

The exaltation of the self has helped to create an altogether unrealistic perspective on what being alive entitles us to have, want, or be. With all its conflict, tension, and anxiety, modern living can never measure up to self-aggrandizing expectations. Cultural disappointment is the underside of cultural narcissism.

Shelley's fateful poem "Ozymandias" reminds us of the perils of self-glorification:

> *I met a traveller from an antique land*
> *Who said: Two vast and trunkless legs of stone*
> *Stand in the desert .... Near them, on the sand,*
> *Half sunk, a shattered visage lies, whose frown,*
> *And wrinkled lip, and sneer of cold command,*
> *Tell that its sculptor well those passions read*
> *Which yet survive, stamped on these lifeless things,*
> *The hand that mocked them, and the heart that fed:*
> *And on the pedestal these words appear:*
> *"My name is Ozymandias, king of kings:*
> *Look on my works, ye Mighty, and despair!"*
> *Nothing beside remains. Round the decay*
> *Of that colossal wreck, boundless and bare*
> *The lone and level sands stretch far away.*

Life According to Madison Avenue

In your field of vision you see a gull circling with effortless grace, floating on the windstream high above the billowing waves of the sea. Sensuous, bewitching music plays in the background, calling you away from everyday cares and responsibilities. Suddenly you are at poolside where an elegant woman clad in a scanty black two-piece lies seductively waiting. But for what? The blue waters of the pool reflect the summer sunshine on her tawny skin. A man, equally elegant and evenly muscled, appears from the other side of the elongated pool. He dives in without disturbing the water's surface, an underwater missile moving directly toward the woman. The music heightens. There is the suggestion he will surface at any moment between her legs. You are waiting for the denouement. Just as suddenly, the music fades and a deep masculine voice is heard speaking in authoritative tones.

A dream, perhaps? Or a fantasy? No, these images are an advertisement for a popular perfume. Unable to provide scent samples to the television audience, the manufacturer has hired an ad agency to "express" the essence of the fragrance through sight and sound, and thereby interest consumers in the product.

The average TV viewer is subject to dozens of these thirty-second spots each day and countless numbers of other advertisements on buses, trains, taxis, billboards, radio, newspapers and now on the internet. No one doubts the powerful nature of these ubiquitous messages. They can make or break a product, sell a political candidate, even foment a revolution. They surround us, hound us, and often astound us, yet it has been very difficult to measure their full impact on our culture. Advertising boosts sales. If we see it touted on TV, we go out and buy it. Is it that simple?

Fundamentally, advertising informs us of available products and services and extols their virtues. It provides us with a haphazard directory of pain remedies, hair dyes, auto manufacturer rebates, light beer. But of course it doesn't stop there. Advertising creates demand. It influences us to want those things for which we had no use until we viewed the ad. As Calvin Coolidge remarked, "Advertising is the method by which the desire is created for better things."

This function is no accident. Mass manufacturing requires consumer interest to sell its wares. Advertising is the tool used to stoke the fire of acquisitive desire. Most successful television advertisements communicate directly by presenting us with a series of images accompanied by mood-enhancing sound. The words dubbed over these scenes are of secondary importance. Pictures are more powerful agents of meaning. In this ad, we are confronted with a lovely and sensuous poolscape. Maybe you've had a hard day at work or just fought with the kids. The ideal representation of life on the screen is attracting and comforting. It transports you from the repetitive and dull rituals of existence to a higher plane. The initial message: "You can have a better life than you have now. Why settle for less?" By presenting ideal representations of existence, free of poverty, illness, death, and responsibility, the ad implies our lives are somehow lacking, thus feeding our dissatisfaction.

Simultaneously, certain valued qualities — in this case physical beauty, sexuality, desirability, and intrigue — are associated with the product. The implication is that if we wear the fragrance, we will somehow attain the promised excitement, desire, and so forth. Thus addicted, consumers buy a brand of cigarettes not on the basis of taste or tar and nicotine content, but on the attributes ascribed to it. One brand is associated with western machismo and individualism, another with the liberated female, a third with detached "hipness." The product itself is not inherently any of these things. It is advertising that has made it so by presenting two contiguous images in order to associate one with the other. Using this basic principle of conditioning we could conceivably sell dog food on the basis of sex or antifreeze on its relationship to leisure. The second message of advertising is: "Buy this product and the traits ascribed to it will transform you."

In a larger sense, advertising is selling not a particular product but consumerism itself as an answer to the human predicament. The third and most inclusive message: "Yes, existence is filled with loneliness, anxiety, boredom, meaninglessness. The way to avoid these discomforts is to surround yourself with all manner of goods. Acquisition is the answer to alienation and misery."

Taken together, the three messages of advertising create a scenario for disappointment:

- Ideal representations distort reality and call our attention to what we don't have. We may feel disappointed when our world doesn't measure up to the "perfect" images that ads present.

- By associating products with valued attributes, ads create false expectations. If we buy the perfume and fail to acquire the associated qualities, we may experience letdown.

- Consumerism does not provide happiness or an answer to the problems inherent in living. We don't reduce our loneliness or anxiety by the purchase of a food processor or a fur coat. By promising a panacea which it cannot deliver, advertising creates false hopes.

Beyond these disappointments, specific advertising themes indirectly create the preconditions for disappointment. Always successful at exploiting cultural trends, ad executives have observed the movement toward narcissism in the culture and are now using the issue of entitlement to appeal to the mass audience in order to sell goods and services. Hence, we are now inundated with the expressed or implied message "You *deserve* only the best."

Why do we allow ourselves to be manipulated? Gullibility, wish fulfillment, avoidance of reality, relief from boredom are all possible explanations. There is little doubt, however, that we would not be such easy prey for the advertising industry if we were more deeply rooted in certainty. In an age of continual technological and social change, when traditional values and mores are in transition, we are left groping for meaning and direction. Under these conditions, snake oil peddlers using glitzy packaging and focus-group-tested promises can snare even the most seasoned individuals. Advertising is the pied piper whom we willingly follow down the road to disappointment.

Media Myths

We live in the information age. Our view of the world is shaped by the data we receive and the manner in which we receive it. Whether its CNN, the internet, the daily newspaper or the six o'clock news, the media link us to a larger community and influence our perception of what is real. Today, virtually any person on the street will concede the powerful role it plays in our lives.

When television became a cultural force in the fifties, most social psychologists thought it would have a revolutionary influence. Having observed the startling effects of propaganda during World War II, they believed TV would make us a nation of homebound, passive drones, living vicariously through the lives of a favorite sitcom or soap hero. As more extensive research was done in the sixties, it became clear that the earliest fears of the social scientists were unfounded. TV and movies were shown, in fact, to have an almost negligible effect on daily living patterns. Subjects ignored messages that ran contrary to existing attitudes and beliefs. The power of the media to influence behavior, studies claimed, had been blown out of proportion.

Sociologist Herbert Gans has labeled these two nascent viewpoints the "hyperdermic" and "selective perception" theories. In the first, the media is seen as freely injecting ideas into an accepting, quiescent public that is highly suggestible. In the second, the audience is viewed as discriminating and impervious. It absorbs information that supports its view of the world and discounts contradicting ideas and values. The hyperdermic position assumes a cause and effect relationship between violence on television and violence in the culture. The selective-perception theory contends that aggressive individuals are more likely to seek out violent programming and that peaceable viewers will not be influenced by it.

While both opposing perspectives have some validity, the truth is hard to nail down. Research indicates that frequently, when watching television and movies, we are selective and critical, taking sharp issue with what we see. Other times, like a dry sponge, we mindlessly absorb the messages that bombard our sense apparatus. How we react depends as much on mood, context, and frequency of exposure as on the message itself.

If the research on behavioral effects is less definitive, what can we say about the influence of the media on something as intangible as expectation or desire? We do know that young children, on seeing commercials for toys and games, express strong wishes for the advertised product. We also know that television and motion pictures, which provide both sight and sound, are very effective tools for learning. Virtually anything, from the alphabet to Greek philosophy, can be taught if there is sufficient attention and proper reinforcement. Can there be any doubt that the media influence our level of material desire and serve as an instrument of learning about life?

Although the media's vision of reality is distorted by the limitations of its technology and the twin requirements to entertain and show a profit, we are surrounded by evidence of its impact on the culture.

Examples: A billion-dollar movie about a mythic ill-fated voyage sends record numbers packing for cruise vacations. The internet, with twenty-four-hour access to information and individuals, changes the design of work and personal relations. An interspace adventure with wondrous visual effects influences the content and direction of imaginary play for two generations of children. As Marshall McLuhan reminds us, the media are extensions of ourselves. They are the functional equivalents of personal experience. Their effects can be immediate or delayed, short- or long-term, direct or indirect. Former Indonesian President Sukarno, quoted in *Variety* years ago, acknowledged the power of film to influence expectation when he declared:

> *The motion picture industry has provided a window on the world, and the colonized nations have looked through that window and have seen the things of which they have been deprived. It is perhaps not generally realized that a refrigerator can be a revolutionary symbol to a people who have no refrigerators. A motor car owned by a worker in one country can be a symbol of revolt to a people deprived of even the necessities of life.... [Hollywood] helped to build up the sense of deprivation of man's birthright, and that sense of deprivation has played a large part in the national revolutions of postwar Asia.*

What Sukarno knew, and what we in America have not given enough notice, is that the media supply a view of material possibility that is eye-opening. To a man from New Guinea, the most memorable scene from a TV series may be the close-up of modern plumbing. In much the same way as advertising, movies and television present us with a cavalcade of desired products and services. We see magnificent houses, landscaped gardens, sailboats, late-model automobiles, appliances of every color and function. In effect, the wide screen is one large free-market commercial. McLuhan agrees:

> *When the movies came, the entire pattern of American life went on the screen as a nonstop ad. Whatever any actor or actress wore or used or ate was such an ad as had never been dreamed of... The result was that all ads in magazines and the press had to look like scenes from a movie. They still do.*

This material array has the power to produce a sense of insufficiency and acquisitive desire that leads to resentment and disappointment with one's own level of accumulated wealth. Where the gap between what is pictured and what is possessed is largest, the dissatisfaction is most keenly felt. In this way, TV and movies function much like advertising. Instead of associating products with a desired attribute, however, they link them to appealing characters with whom we can identify. When the heroine escapes in her Porsche, tires screaming, the car's image is enhanced, as is the viewer's desire to own one.

Beyond the advertising effect, TV and motion pictures act in other ways to produce disappointment. Hollywood and major networks are business enterprises that need to produce films and programs that will draw at the box office and score well on the Nielsen ratings. To accomplish this goal, they use themes that appeal to the interest and concerns of a mass audience. Universal issues that transcend class, regional, or cultural barriers are favored. Over the years the media has learned that it is both entertaining and profitable to exploit the richness of American myths — those popular collective beliefs based more on how we wish the world were than the way it really is. Earlier I wrote of these desires as profound lifewishes for glamour, excitement, fairness, romance, love, safety, freedom, and so forth.

A blockbuster film about the uphill battle of a club fighter gave birth to four sequels because it appealed to our wish for the victory of the underdog against great odds. At last, the wide screen delivered what the real world would not: justice and a happy ending. Soap operas have moved into prime-time television slots because they are emotional tar pits supplying vicarious interpersonal excitement. They offer an amplified slice of life, exorbitant and overstated but satisfying in its appeal to our wish for drama and the destruction of the archvillain. Even the westerns — masquerading in their current form as cop shows — have been a mainstay of both TV and movies because they create the perfect context for a morality play. They indulge our wish for a benevolent father who wins out over the forces of anarchy and chaos.

In perpetuating these myths, the media pamper our illusions and distort our world view. Of course, some of what we ingest will be spit out as fraudulent or pure fantasy in accordance with the "selective perception" hypothesis. But a great deal more will sink into the holding tank of the unconscious. Given the number of hours Americans spend in front of the "tube" and the ever-increasing attendance records at local cinemas, this seepage is inevitable. To paraphrase a modern adage, "You are what you watch."

It's not that Hollywood and the networks implant illusions and myths in our collective psyche. They simply play to the already existing wishful notions acquired in childhood. The dangers are obvious. Life can never match the wide screen for romance and drama. If in our daily living we expect "to live happily ever after" or "see the bad guy get his just deserts," we can almost count on feeling disappointed. The pseudo-reality of the media gratifies our wishes and distorts our sense of possibility.

One of my patients, a generally cautious twenty-nine-year-old civil engineer, commented on the connection between his unsuccessful relationship and the movies:

> *I expected her to be flawless, larger than life. And I thought we were playing out a great drama like you see in the movies. Boy meets girl. They fall in love and, in spite of the odds, overcome the impossible. They do what everyone else says can't be done.*
>
> *But it didn't happen. When I look back I see that even after the first week there were problems. I just didn't want to face them. I wanted it to be like a Hollywood story. Reality just caught up with us.*

Aside from exploiting our lifewishes, the media influence expectation in more subtle ways. Have you ever noticed that on the screen the hero never shines his shoes or flosses his teeth? Neither does the heroine hem a skirt or return spoiled merchandise to the supermarket. The commonplace events of modern life so necessary for survival are rarely shown on film except in the *cinema verite* or as a backdrop to make a point about loneliness or boredom. Life is portrayed in highlights without the duller moments that make up most of experience.

Let us say, for example, that we see a film about a boy and his dog. We leave the theater feeling unaffected. The theme is too sentimental and trite; the myths on which the story revolves, too mawkish. At the same time that we are consciously repudiating the film's influence, we are viewing a drama that has a beginning, middle, and end; that builds to a climax and finds resolution; that is observed from the outside by an omniscient observer. The structure of the film — if not the content — affects our view of reality.

Daily living does not follow such a neat course. It is often difficult to recognize a beginning amid the myriad of events that transpire at any given time. Endings, too, are frequently over-looked. Only the ritualized demarcations, often lacking in spontaneity, receive attention (weddings, funerals, and so forth). Likewise, the dramatic denouement so necessary to the unraveling of the plot is missing in real life. There is rarely an evenly developed crescendo of events which clearly resolves itself. Real life is messy, unpredictable, and sometimes problems drag on interminably without solution or closure.

Art imitates life, but it is also a fact in this media age that the reverse is true. We mimic our art forms and distort reality in doing so. Film and television present a vision of possibility that is perfect — observable, dramatic, faultless. Real life, on the other hand, although at times dramatic, is generally mundane, flawed, and ambiguous. Events proceed without the control of an accomplished director. There are no retakes, no editing, and no easy moral lessons. The media beckon us to see the world in their particular way. By expecting our lives to mirror the clarity, order, and histrionics of television and motion pictures, we create the preconditions for disappointment. Our challenge is to maintain sensible expectations in the face of exorbitancy.

Chronic
Disappointment Styles

Introduction

Disappointment patterns are built into the structure of the psyche. Biological endowments and personal history determine the attitudes, beliefs, and patterns of adaptation that make up a particular personality. These enduring traits, which vary little with time or place, influence the nature of expectation. Whether one maintains romantic, idealized, or impossibly high hopes has as much to do with character as it does with the specifics of each situation. The essential quality of one's disappointment, therefore, must also be affected by personality.

For example, a woman is brought up to think her value is determined solely by her level of accomplishment. In order to maintain a sense of worth, she believes she must set rigid, perfectionistic goals for herself. She has to be the best at everything she does, and she applies these requirements to her children, spouse, and friends as well. Her perfectionism gives all her disappointments a singular flavor. She can't understand why others are always letting her down.

Some personalities are more likely to experience disappointment than others. In the following three chapters I present the acquiescent, deprived, and self-important styles. Each is prone to a particular, chronic form of disappointment that reflects the deeper issues of character.

Chapter 6

The Acquiescent Style

*I am not in this world to live up to your
expectations. And you are not in this world
to live up to mine.*

— Fritz Perls

ileen is the co-director of a childcare center in the inner
city. She is a small woman, in her early thirties, married for
the last eight years to a physician. People who meet her for
the first time are struck by her reticence. She is shy, with a round,
youthful face that gives her an innocent appearance. Her eyes in
particular draw attention. They seem to say, "I'll do anything to please
but I'm afraid it won't be enough." She wears loose-fitting clothing
which disguises the lines of her figure and might be better suited to
a larger, older person. Her manner is mildly deferential, consistent
with her view of herself as a cooperative, moral individual.

Eileen can't remember the last time she expressed hostility or
anger. She is usually described as a "giving person," well-liked by
friends and coworkers. Rarely does she utter an unkind word. On
the contrary, she consistently suppresses any negative feelings of

envy, competition, or ill-will. In all arenas of her life, she works hard to do the "right" thing and win the approval of others. At work, Eileen puts in long hours to make certain the daycare center runs smoothly. At home, she is a dutiful and attentive wife. With her parents and friends she is always more than willing to give of herself and rarely asks for anything in return.

A work experience typifies her character. About a week before the spring open house, a major event at the daycare center, the other co-director approached her with a problem. Her parents were coming to town during the busy week, and she had promised to take them traveling around the area. This visit was important to her. Would Eileen mind if she took the week off? Without hesitation or complaint, Eileen agreed, although she recognized with fleeting resentment that she would be left to plan, set up, and run the open house alone. By the end of the hectic period, she was exhausted and had caught a bad cold. She had sacrificed her well-being to meet someone else's needs. Yet such action was not uncommon for her. In spite of her fatigue and physical condition, she would do it again.

Curiously, Eileen's selfless actions do not seem to influence the way she feels about herself. Despite positive feedback from her friends, she continues to experience feelings of worthlessness and inadequacy. Always dissatisfied with her level of accomplishment, she sees herself as second-best, never quite good enough, regardless of how hard she tries. Her self-critical attitude causes her to be persistently disappointed in herself.

Eileen's story illustrates a specific relationship to disappointment which I call the "acquiescent style." Unlike other patterns overloaded with unrealistic expectations of one's choosing, acquiescent individuals are smothered by the expectations of others. The heart of the problem is one impossible requirement: to meet all the demands — real or imagined — of others. It is a Sisyphian task without hope of success. But this does not deter these compliant personalities. They struggle to achieve the impossible, ultimately trading their own well-being for transitory approval. Disappointment in self is common among such individuals. They feel inadequate and undermined because they respond not from their own inner needs, but from their desire to please. Even when they succeed, they fail. The process of continually trying to measure up to others' expectations separates them from their own sense of self.

Eileen's psychological past tells us how this sort of pattern emerges. As the younger of two children and the only daughter in a comfortable suburban household, she formed a strong and early bond with her mother, whom she described as "a housewife with few interests other than her family." Her mother was intimately involved in the daily regimen of Eileen's life. She drove her to ballet class, singing lessons, and to friends' houses after school. From age six, her mother regularly visited her bedroom in the evening to talk with her. Eileen shared her deepest feelings about herself, school, and friends. Mother confided her feelings of loneliness and doubts about her troubled relationship with her husband, who was rarely at home. Eileen had mixed feelings about these nightly talks. She enjoyed her special role as confidante but sometimes felt burdened by the responsibility. There were uncomfortable moments when she wanted to exclude her mother from parts of her life, but didn't, to avoid hurting her.

Mother selected Eileen's clothing, helped her with her homework, guided her friendships, directed her relationships with boys, and counseled her about the future. She was interested in every facet of her daughter's life and encouraged her with extravagant praise whenever she lived up to her standards.

It's strange, but unlike my friends I never fought with my mother. I always assumed she was doing her best for me. Fighting with her always made me feel wrong. One time she didn't like a friend I had made at school. I remember how guilty I felt about ignoring this person, and to please my mother, I broke off the friendship just like that. I felt I couldn't afford to lose my mother. She was my best friend.

Eileen's father, an orthopedic surgeon, was always at the hospital. During her childhood their relationship was tenuous. She feared and respected him but she never felt close. In adolescence this pattern began to change as they spent more time together. They would take long drives in the country during which she chronicled the daily events of her life. He listened quietly, occasionally commenting on something she had said or criticizing her failures and admonishing her to do better. She looked up to him as the ideal man — powerful, responsible, and exacting. He liked things his way and would not tolerate deviance or rebellion. In these adolescent years, his opinion was a primary concern of hers. She always tried to please, dreading his reproach. His fault-finding nature scared her, yet she was equally determined to win him over.

In contrast to her older brother, who was always getting into trouble, Eileen was considered by everyone to be a "good girl." Her teachers liked her, and she did well in school. She dated the "right" boys, participated in the "proper" activities, and was the sort of child mothers would point out as exemplary. At times, this made her uncomfortable with her peers, but she also experienced her "rightness" as a source of pride.

In describing her childhood and adolescence, Eileen could not recall a single incident in which she had been in conflict with her parents or an authority figure. In fact, she was rarely involved in conflicts even with her friends. She was scared by her brother's freewheeling style and advised him to stop bringing embarrassment to his parents, "who had given him so much."

When the time came for Eileen to consider college (there was never any doubt she would go), she flirted with the idea of attending a large university in another state. On her parents' advice, she chose a local school. Wanting to be near her family, she persuaded herself that just as good an education could be had close to home as far away. She lived with her parents, and the next four years were a safe and comfortable extension of her high school experience.

In her senior year she began dating a medical student who seemed like a perfect partner for her. He was practical, dependable, and high-minded, and he knew where he was going. His certainty attracted her immediately, and three months after she graduated, they married. Her parents naturally had approved of her choice, and the young couple moved into an apartment found by her mother.

> *In many ways, when I first met Tim he reminded me of my father — very serious and a little aloof. I wouldn't say we had a romance. Basically, we liked each other and were comfortable relating, but there was no courtship. It just seemed to happen. And when we decided to get married, it was the most practical decision. My parents really liked him, and I could see him fitting into the family. He and my father had a lot to talk about.*

By Eileen's own admission, their marriage paralleled that of her parents. Tim was away long hours, and she found herself with little to do. Tim maintained his distance and Eileen, who had seen this kind of arrangement all her life, never thought to question it. Tim played the "top dog" role, offering frequent criticism and admonishment. Eileen assumed the compliant position, anxious to please, but never quite measuring up. She began to feel more disappointed in herself as she failed to satisfy him. Despite her fears about looking for work, she saw the need to develop independent interests. She got a real ego-boost when she found a job teaching part time in a preschool. When the co-director spot at the adjoining daycare center was vacated, her self-doubts at first kept her from applying. Was she capable of managing an entire agency? The only way to find out was to try. Yet she feared a blow to her fledgling self-esteem. Uncharacteristically, she took the risk and was hired after the first interview.

The Loss of Inner Direction

Eileen's personal history reflects the dominant role her parents played in her life. As friend, confidante, advisor, and nurturer, Eileen's mother had a hand in all her daughter's affairs. No unconventional thoughts were encouraged, no privacy tolerated. Every inner pang, every deep feeling was shared under the guise of love and concern. Even when Eileen felt the need to maintain her distance, she experienced guilt for not being completely open with her parents. Such a profound involvement creates either an enmeshed relationship that stifles individual development toward autonomy or an unhealthy overidentification with the mother that undermines the child's ability to make self-determined choices.

By intruding on every aspect of Eileen's life, her mother took from her the opportunity to both succeed and fail on her own. It is through this trial-and-error experience that children learn the satisfaction of mastery and build confidence.

Eileen believed that if she expressed preferences that were different from her mother's, she would in fact be hurting her "best friend." Experience had taught her that when she said no or opposed her mother's direction, their relationship suffered. Love was withdrawn. Self-assertion was therefore associated with injuring her mother, a circumstance a good daughter would do anything to avoid. In effect, her behavior was ruled by the dictum, "Since she does everything for me, I cannot very well refuse her. And if I do, she will be hurt." It is clear that such an arrangement sacrifices the child's pressing need for self-direction in order to meet the requirements of someone else.

Approval Is the Number-One Priority

Eileen's mother was sweet and loving as long as her daughter acted in ways she thought best. The message Eileen understood was "Be a good girl or I won't love you." But beyond that withdrawal of love, Eileen was motivated by the additional pressure of guilt. When she was not "good," she was led to believe she had actually injured her mother in some important way. This produced feelings of wrongness which persuasively influenced her to bring her behavior into line. Losing love was bad enough; hurting Mom was intolerable.

Eileen's dependence on approval-seeking behavior was equaled only by her avoidance of disapproval. Her relationship with her father reflected this process. She would seek his point of view and find herself expressing it to her friends as if it were her own. She dated boys she was not particularly interested in because they were acceptable to him. But in her compliant behavior she was also attempting to avoid his criticism — his sideways glance, furrowed brow, or chastising tone. These hurt her more than failure to win his approval through correct actions. What seemed like straightforward attempts to win acceptance were actually ploys to avoid disapproval.

Living Other People's Expectations

Eileen's life expectations were identical with her parents' because in fact they were borrowed from them. In learning to be the perfect daughter she had forgotten what she wanted for herself. She was living their script and acting in their play.

Eileen found that all her relationships reflected these early patterns. With her peers she was always anxious to please. Her schoolwork was a constant attempt to meet the expectations of her teachers. In new situations she would think to herself, "How does this person want me to be?" She tailored her behavior to fit what she believed was the expectation. These responses were not processed consciously. In fact, the only time she was aware of this pattern was when she failed to win someone's approval or affection.

In her marriage she tried to please her husband, win his love and approval, and avoid his censure. If he wanted a dutiful wife —a supportive, passive, domestic type — then that's what she would be. If he preferred an intellectual peer or a charming companion to wear on his arm, she would work hard to be those things. Occasionally she resented this endless pressure and her husband as well, but these singular moments were usually followed by periods of self-reproach for failing to be what he wanted.

Work was no different. Her behavior was shaped by the expectations of her boss, the board of directors, and especially her staff. Her constant endeavor to please everyone was only partially successful. And the effort was exhausting.

Because she was afraid of disappointing, she found it difficult to use the authority inherent in her administrative position. She could not say "no" or draw the line when necessary. Her "good girl" training did not prepare her for assertive behavior, and she was afraid of appearing harsh or arbitrary. As long as she had no power, her compliant tendencies were only a nuisance. Put in a position of authority, she felt paralyzed.

Disappointment in Self

To the question "What do you want?" Eileen could barely respond. After thirty-one years, she was still trying to please, still trying to measure up to the expectations of others. In truth she did not know what she wanted because her focus had always been away from herself. This external orientation left her a stranger to her own needs and preferences, and, in a broader sense, to her own nature. Without someone else to react to she was lost. In brief periods of introspection she always felt empty and disappointed in herself. Her solution was to try harder to be the good daughter, the perfect boss, the ideal wife. But these efforts were counterproductive. They never changed her deep-seated feelings.

Eileen was disappointed in herself for failing to meet the demands of those around her. She was attempting to live her life like a novice painter who merely colors in the outlines drawn by someone else. There is no inspiration in such an exercise. It is prosaic and spiritless. No wonder she experienced disappointment.

When Eileen felt resentment toward others for their demands, real or imagined, she censored those feelings and turned them back on herself. So afraid was she of her own accumulated anger that she converted it to disappointment in self as a means of avoiding its expression. Thus, instead of venting anger at her mother for expecting a daily telephone call, Eileen condemned herself. "If I were a good daughter," she thought, "I wouldn't resent calling her."

To some extent, her self-disappointment was also a reflection of her parents' response when she had failed to satisfy them as a child. In effect, she had "internalized" their reaction and was now playing their former roles in her own drama. She was both "disappointing" and "disappointed." Convoluted as this turnaround may seem at first glance, it is quite common. The admonishing voice of our parents remains within us long after we separate from them. It becomes our own reproving inner surrogate, advising us that we should have known better, tried harder, and so forth. In the language of transactional analysis, this voice is the "critical parent"; in psychoanalysis, the superego; in religion, the conscience. Whatever we call the judgmental arbiter, it carries the stamp of our parents' particular fault-finding style. If they expressed anger at our failings, we will likely use the same tactic on ourselves. If they showed letdown ... well, the result is obvious. For Eileen, dissatisfaction in self was the flip side of her parents' disappointment in her.

The Acquiescent Style in Retrospect

The acquiescent style is based on one desire: to meet the expectations of other people. When put this simply, such behavior sounds foolish and absurd. But due to the circumstances of their personal histories, compliant individuals come to believe that the approval of others is a necessary ingredient in their interpersonal lives. Without approval they doubt themselves and feel directionless. Yet seeking validation exclusively from others undermines their integrity and sense of self. They lose both ways.

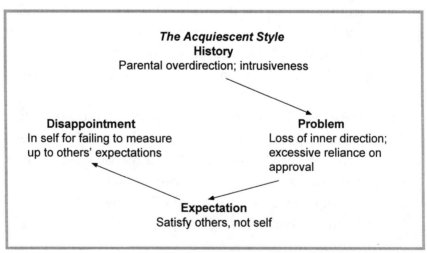

The Acquiescent Style
History
Parental overdirection; intrusiveness

Disappointment
In self for failing to measure up to others' expectations

Problem
Loss of inner direction; excessive reliance on approval

Expectation
Satisfy others, not self

This style inevitably results in disappointment because one cannot please all the people all the time. It is difficult enough to meet one's own expectations. Compliant individuals, trying to accomplish the impossible, end up pleasing no one, especially not themselves. It is a self-defeating and self-perpetuating pattern of behavior which ends in despair. As with all disappointment, prevention requires reevaluation of the basic expectation and the lifewish underlying it. The profound desire to be loved unconditionally characterizes all acquiescent personalities. Because approval was historically linked to "correct" behavior, they long for acceptance and affection with no strings attached. Feeling unworthy of such love, they are trapped. Since they believe they can only win the validating affection of others through pleasing and compliant behavior, they can never find the unqualified acceptance they crave. Giving up the lifewish to be loved unconditionally and risking disapproval by taking independent action according to internal needs provides the exit from this impasse.

Disappointing Others

A variant on the acquiescent style is the individual who is always disappointing others. Much like Eileen, this person has been raised in an overdirected environment characterized by high expectation and parental manipulation through the display and withdrawal of love. But where Eileen attempted to meet many of these expectations (and was sometimes successful), disappointing individuals do not. They consistently let other people down, rarely coming through at the critical moment and frustrating all who depend on them. It is as if their behavior is saying, "You see, I told you not to expect anything from me."

Examples: The spouse who retreats whenever demands are placed on him; the daughter who consistently fails to show up for important family events; the contractor who repeatedly promises to meet a deadline and never delivers.

These disappointing individuals are of two types: active and passive. Actives cover their tracks by offering inflated assurances they have little intention of honoring. Passives hide from all commitments whenever they can get away with it. The difference is one of style. Both types feel incapable of meeting life's demands. Too burdened, angry, or thwarted, they have historically been unable to satisfy the expectations of their parents, and this view of themselves as "disappointing children" has marked them. Rather than risk failing in their efforts, they choose not to make the attempt, hence insuring a continuing style of failure followed by feelings of deficiency. Ironically, such individuals fear success as much as failure since the former brings with it expectations of continued mastery.

Most of these disappointing individuals find little comfort in their familiar ne'er-do-well role but they have little impetus for change. By throwing off the cloak of others' expectations through their repeated failure to come through, they have created a safe but unsatisfying niche for themselves: no one realistically expects anything from them. They have fulfilled their childhood "script" to perfection.

Chapter 7

The Deprived Style

A child forsaken, waking suddenly,
Whose gaze afeard on all things round doth rove,
And seeth only that it cannot see
The meeting eyes of love.
— George Eliot

Expect the worst! Catastrophe, loss, disease, humiliation, anticipate them all. Think of the blessed relief you'll experience should the outcome be more favorable. And if it is not, at least you'll be prepared for any contingency. This is the strategy of the person who has been severely wounded by disappointment in childhood. He or she walks through the world hoping to avoid a repetition of history by anticipating the negative event. The chosen remedy is unfortunate because it distorts perception. Expecting a piano to fall on your head tends to put quite a crook in the neck. You can't see straight anymore. Always looking skyward, you lose perspective, swept up by fears and wariness. Comedian George Burns humorously described such a person as "a man who feels bad when he feels good for fear he'll feel worse when he feels better."

You probably know people like this. Pessimism is the only perspective that feels comfortable to them because their thinking is based on two incorrigible premises: "Life is pain" and "You never get what you want." Although their world view is ostensibly focused on preventing disappointment, they are profoundly disillusioned. Their nihilism is a defense against ever being hurt or let down. So deep and early is the original disappointment that the individual's perspective is terribly tainted by childhood history. To risk disappointment is to possibly reconnect with the primary pain of the past, a possibility feared above all others. I call this pattern of disappointment the "deprived style" because it reflects the individual's most basic feeling about life.

Peter's Story

Peter, a heavy-drinking, forty-five-year-old architect, has a clever, acerbic wit, with a bitterness so palpable it is nearly contagious. After twelve years of putting up with his sarcasm, his wife announced her desire for a divorce. At first he protested with all his characteristic irony, but when she began dating other men, he reluctantly acceded to her request. After their separation, he drew into himself, took to drinking in the afternoons, and relinquished all pleasurable activity. He became despairing and world-weary, describing himself as "jaded and bummed out." He gave the impression of being considerably older than his actual age. With the death of his ambition and no clear life goals, his only concern was getting through the day. He and his wife had no children. He rarely saw his family, who lived two thousand miles away. He was a man alone, who seemed —at least for the moment —to want to keep it that way.

To the observing eye, Peter appeared frail, as if his level of energy were insufficient to meet the stress of living. His legs in particular looked spindly and weak, offering his torso only marginal support. His feet were bony and narrow, creating the same impression. His facial skin was sallow and drawn. His body was elongated and thin, and his musculature seemed underdeveloped in general. When he stood up, his shoulders stooped and his chest collapsed into itself. He seemed to have difficulty standing firmly on his own two feet.

Further observation revealed that Peter hardly exerted himself when breathing. His respiration was shallow. He inhaled and exhaled in a tentative manner and his torso showed minimal movement. His eyes held a longing, soulful expression with a slight trace of acrimony. There was a stubborn quality to his set jaw. He looked like a man who willed himself through difficult times by the sheer power of his defiance. His body was rock-hard, as if shaped by loneliness and deprivation.

Peter's feelings about himself supported these impressions. He believed no one could be trusted: "Sooner or later they turn on you or abandon you for greener pastures." He was bitter about his wife's treatment of him, but his attitude was resigned: "What can you expect? Relationships are just arrangements in which people use each other until they become bored and split. It's inevitable." From Peter's point of view it made no sense to express feelings even if he could muster them. Your partner would simply use the information against you at another time. "We don't really need anyone else but ourselves," he would say. "We carry around this myth that we must be surrounded by other people when, in fact, we can get along perfectly well alone." And, of course, Peter's life of isolation was penetrated by few friends and no intimates. He had modest material and interpersonal needs, and managed where others couldn't because he required so little. And he expected even less from life. He anticipated the worst and usually got it. His vision of the world as a bleak landscape devoid of tenderness was self-fulfilling. He had it all figured out. But he was miserable and drinking himself into oblivion.

At first glance, Peter's difficulties seem merely a poor adjustment to his wrecked marriage. But his history reveals that he was not simply reacting to the pain of current bruises. He had struggled his whole life with the enduring pain of isolation and disappointment. His present situation was a mirror of his past.

A Loveless Childhood

The fourth and last child of immigrant parents, Peter was born at an inopportune time. Shortly after his birth, his father's small store went bankrupt, and his mother was forced to find employment to supplement the family income. Peter's oldest sister took care of him indifferently, leaving him alone for long periods. His older brother bullied him while his parents ignored his urgent protests. He had the impression, in fact, that they thought he complained too much, and after a while he gave up seeking their intervention. He felt isolated within the family and felt especially neglected by his mother, who was always too busy to look after his needs. Once she had failed to come to a play in which he had a principal role. He was heartbroken, but did not even mention the event when he came home.

To deal with his sense of deprivation and loss, Peter created a fantasy world with over a dozen nurturing and adoring characters. He gave himself in fantasy what he was unable to find in his family. Because be had received such minimal affection and care, he found himself looking everywhere for signs of reassurance. He described himself as a clinging and dependent child. He followed his sisters around but was usually ostracized by them. His brother simply used him as a target for his own frustrations.

Peter's memory of the past was startlingly clear and fresh. He remembered dozens of incidents in which he had felt emotionally hurt. He recalled the hand-me-down clothes from his brother and cousins, which were always too big and made him feel insignificant. He thought of the numerous promises made by his parents that were never kept. He remembered things not with hurt and longing, but in a detached manner as if they were the events of someone else's life. His stoicism was understandable but seemed out of place.

By age ten Peter had ceased his clinging behavior and had withdrawn further into himself. He no longer followed his sisters or bothered his brother. He rarely asked for anything. He began to take a certain pride in needing less than his siblings. He felt righteous in his independence. His parents implied that they considered his new behavior constructive and a sign of maturity. At school he maintained his isolation. He felt different from his peers. Although he acted calm and in control, he really felt overwhelmed and afraid. He confided in no one.

Adolescence brought only minor changes in this pattern. He remained isolated and began to develop skills in the fine arts. He spent long hours sketching pictures of men in boxes and figures reaching out into space. These wonderfully detailed drawings expressed his deepest feelings. The boxes represented the sense of enclosed isolation that separated him from others. Reaching out reflected his deep need to make contact despite the barriers he experienced around him.

Relationships with the opposite sex were also difficult. Peter seemed to find himself struggling continually with unrequited love affairs. He sought out young women who were not interested in him and pined away, writing poems and sketching their faces. Peter rejected those who paid him any attention. If they were interested in him, how desirable could they be? Following the classic Groucho line, "I wouldn't join any club that would have me as a member," he discounted potential partners on the basis of their poor taste. He was undesirable. They must be too.

Peter chose to pursue a career as an architect. In his early adulthood, he worked very hard to perfect his craft. This was done at the expense of a personal life. He continued to remain aloof, although he had many business acquaintances whom he counted among his friends. In his early thirties he met Lisa, who worked in the office of one of his associates. He struck up a friendship immediately, but it was she who pursued him. After two years they decided to marry. It was the sort of relationship that outsiders considered ideal. They shared the same profession, a devotion to their work, and similar lifestyles. Their temperaments were also alike — low-keyed and mild. Not as apparent was the paucity of affection they gave each other. Self-disclosure was rare, and sharing feelings of vulnerability inconceivable. They were emotionally distant "intimate" partners. Over the years the distance between them grew. Finally, aware of the irreparable gap between them, Lisa made a last attempt to reach out to him. She asked that they see a marriage and family therapist together. Peter acknowledged their problem but refused counseling, unwilling to change the way he related to her. For him, intimate contact was painful, risky, and unfamiliar. Eventually they separated. Lisa found another partner. Peter withdrew further into himself.

The Broken Heart

Infancy is a time of great vulnerability. Lying on its back, unable to turn its tiny body or even raise its head to look at the new world, the newborn is a study in helplessness. It relies entirely on the care and nurturance of its parents. If there is some profound disturbance or pattern of abuse in the contact or nursing of the infant, its sense of well-being is compromised. The effect of that disruption — if it is intense — will ripple through all the developmental stages of the child and into adulthood.

For the young child, bodily connection to the mother is a manifestation of maternal love. To be held is to be protected and nurtured. Although we lack all the details of his early history, there is reason to believe that Peter suffered some sort of interruption in the early nurturing phase. When his mother went to work, his care was entrusted to his oldest sister, who found the task burdensome. He was prematurely expected to look after himself. His sense of deprivation left him empty and disconsolate. Did anyone really care? If he left home, would his family even bother to search for him? Would anyone miss him? In truth, Peter suffered from a broken heart.

Building Walls as a Lifestyle

Peter made peace with his deprivation by denying his needs. This was strategy for survival. He had been bitterly disappointed time and again. In order to diminish his pain and prevent its recurrence, he removed himself from the cause of his troubles: his own needs. If he required nothing, he could not be disappointed. It was a simple solution for which he paid dearly, but it was the most effective and, perhaps, the only viable remedy open to him.

What began as a psychological defense against disappointment and loss became a lifestyle. Eventually Peter began to lose access to his deeper feelings. To avoid further pain he closed off his heart. He thought of love as cheap sentiment or a euphemism for sex. He was able to relate only on the most superficial level. Intimacy was out of the question. This is why his marriage ultimately failed. He would not allow another person in, afraid his neediness would be overwhelming. If he were rejected, the old feelings of deprivation and loss might be reawakened. He preferred a relationship without risk, a passionless and utilitarian arrangement that would be convenient for both parties.

Peter's life was filled with the idiosyncrasies of self-denial. Whereas in the past his parents had been the agents of his deprivation, now, ironically, he chose to deny himself. The deprived identity became an ingrained behavioral pattern. He drove an old car that was always breaking down, even though he could afford something more reliable. He lived in a crowded studio apartment which barely permitted him space for a drafting table. He rarely bought himself anything of value and continued to wear old, shabby clothing except at work. Money was not the issue. Peter just felt uncomfortable providing for himself Anything beyond bare-bones necessity he considered indulgent.

The pattern carried over into other areas. He never allowed himself pleasurable experiences. He took vacations infrequently. It would never occur to him to plan a weekend at a resort or spend a night on the town. He avoided situations that might give him recognition or praise. These experiences made him feel uncomfortable and awkward. He did not know how to respond to compliments or acknowledgments. On one occasion, he left a community meeting early because he suspected a friend was going to praise him publicly for work he had done. It was not humility that drove him away, but rather anxiety with any form of acclamation.

All of Peter's actions were designed to avoid the possibility of further disappointment, the hallmark of the deprived style. (A graphic representation of his experience is shown on page 117.)

Underlying the negative expectation is the lifewish never to be hurt again. But beyond this defensive wish looms a greater and more urgent desire: to get all one's emotional needs met without having to risk asking. Gratification of this unconscious fantasy represents an "undoing" of the deprivation experience by providing the individual with unsolicited nurturance, solid proof that he or she is deserving of the love so long denied. Deprived persons do not dare allow this thought into consciousness because recognition calls up the pain of having been unloved. The defensive wish and expectation is, therefore, substituted as a safer alternative, an attempt to avoid any further disappointment.

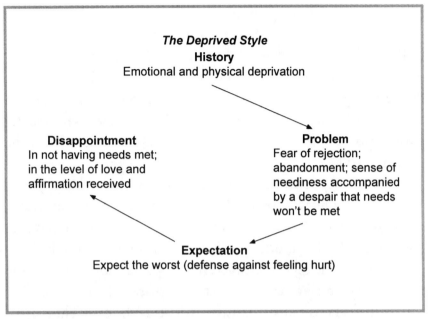

The Deprived Style
History
Emotional and physical deprivation

Disappointment
In not having needs met;
in the level of love and
affirmation received

Problem
Fear of rejection;
abandonment; sense of
neediness accompanied
by a despair that needs
won't be met

Expectation
Expect the worst (defense against feeling hurt)

To move out of this self-perpetuating pattern, these individuals must acknowledge their profound need for love and risk asserting it. They must reach out to others despite deep fears of rejection, and in this way learn that they can survive the ravages of disappointment. Only by taking this chance can they find the caring and affection that has eluded them for so long.

Another Deprived Style: The Romantic

Emotional deprivation in the attachment between parent and child does not always create an individual who expects the worst. Another defense can be used. In response to the deprived condition, the child may indulge in extensive fantasy, reordering the universe in a more tolerable manner. As the individual grows, he or she maintains these fantasies in the culturally acceptable form of romantic or idealistic beliefs. Naturally, not everyone with romantic notions fits into this group. Impassioned thoughts may be the product of uncommon personal traits: For example, a highly developed imagination or a marked sensitivity to the environment. There are those, however, whose very character is built on a longing for life to fulfill idealized myths, the dreamy-eyed souls who hold fast to their storybook perspective in the face of obvious contradicting facts. Such individuals are constantly let down when events fall short of their sentimental anticipations. They show a pattern of disappointment I call the romantic style.

Examples of romantic notions: "And it all ended happily ever after"; "Someone will come along and save me from the mess I've made of my life"; "Love is all one needs"; "I don't have to compromise"; "My mother really loved me in her own way."

The romantic style is characterized by a histrionic view of the world in which all aspects of relationship are colored by passion and ardor. These individuals are in love with love. They crave experiences in which the heart palpitates with feverish desire or longing and they indulge in ill-fated love affairs which leave them in paroxysms of regret. They expect their partners to share their flammable feelings and are prone to cling to their anguish long after a relationship has ended. To people who never got enough love, that four-letter word is magical. Their lives are quests to gain this treasure, but feeling fundamentally undeserving and fearful of attachment, they sabotage intimacy. Their lifewish is for true love to save them — the obvious antidote to the unbearable deprivation of early life. When it does not happen, they seem to relish their tragic condition.

The life expectations of the romantic lean heavily on the themes of cruel fate, the loneliness and purity of isolation, and, above all, the redemption of love. Filled with hyperbole and melodrama, these unrealistic anticipations are futile. Romantic individuals are, therefore, continually disappointed. But a tragic world view is so vital to their sense of identity that they are usually unwilling to adapt to a more grounded approach to life. It is as if they are addicted to the deprivation and yearning pattern begun in their first few years. Its anguished overtones sustain them and they are drawn to the martyr role that accompanies their suffering. They clearly prefer disappointment to the loss of their passion.

The romantic perspective, entrenched as it is in the dual sensibilities of love and tragedy, makes for good reading. Indeed, literature overflows with tales of unrequited love, twists of fate, and forsaken hearts. For that matter, so do the soap operas. But the style is ill-suited for living because it produces excessive expectations. Eventually these extravagant anticipations create enough chronic disappointment to threaten the romantic soul which thrives on adversity. When this happens, depression and despair follow.

Chapter 8

The Self-Important Style

Self-love is the greatest of all flatterers.
— Francois, Duc de La Rochefoucauld

J an and Jonathan are Generation X professionals with graduate degrees, employed in good jobs, materially comfortable, enviably attractive and intelligent, and in good health. Yet, despite their good fortune, they leave the impression that they are deeply disappointed in their lives.

Jonathan: *I know I'm better off than the average manager who may be downsized tomorrow, but somehow that doesn't make me feel better. Jan and I have been working our butts off for a half-dozen years now and we are still struggling to get what we always assumed we'd have. Even with two incomes, we can't afford a house in the city. I'm working as hard as my father did without nearly as much to show for it.*

Jan: *I grew up in an affluent suburb where all my friends went to camp, every family had two cars and a maid, and all the kids had access to their mothers' credit cards. I expected at least the same for myself. True, I have a nice* *apartment, but it's really too small. I'd like to buy a second place in the country but can only afford the land without the house. I'm not even sure I want a child because the cost of good daycare and private school education is so prohibitive.*

Don't get me wrong. Jonathan and I are not poor. We can manage without scrimping. But we both work hard and don't have much to show for it. It doesn't seem fair. With taxes and daily expenses, we can't afford the extras that we're entitled to.

Disappointment in the level of material acquisition is only part of their story. Jan complains of "anonymity" in her huge law firm, "retarded advancement," and lack of genuine recognition for "the blood-and-guts sacrifices I've made." Jonathan resents "being lost" in the government bureaucracy and the lack of acknowledgment by his superiors.

Jonathan: *I don't like being just a number. I want people to notice my efforts and not shrug me off as another guy who puts in forty a week. The worst thing about working in the public sphere is that individuals are taken for granted. They're interchangeable parts.*

When I first began working, fresh out of graduate school with some pretty decent ideas, I thought I would set the place on fire. But as it turned out, no one in a position of power wanted to use them or even try them out on a small scale. Since then I've learned not to waste my energy, but it still galls me.

Jan: *I seem to be moving up through the ranks at work at about the same speed as everyone else. That's what bothers me. I want to be acknowledged for my energies and talents. It's only natural that you want to be seen as someone special.*

Jan's and Jonathan's complaints seem legitimate enough. But if we look a little deeper, we find that their story is more complex. Both Jan and Jonathan fit into a third type of disappointment pattern, the self-important style. These individuals view themselves as special and therefore different from others. They expect the world to recognize their uniqueness and to treat them accordingly. When it invariably does not, they are surprised and resentful. Having grown up in families that encouraged their entitlement, they dislike being mere faces in the crowd. They are obsessed with fantasies of unlimited success, power and brilliance, and their worst fear is that they will live undistinguished lives of little import. They crave attention and exaggerate their achievements and abilities, often displaying arrogant and haughty attitudes.

One-Sided Relationships

Nowhere is the self-important style so problematic as in relationships which require mutuality and shared affection to survive. Self-important individuals have great difficulty establishing a reciprocal arrangement with their partners. They are used to being on top, exercising prerogatives, and receiving favored treatment. They are prone to establish one-sided "instrumental" relationships, viewing their lovers as the source of their narcissistic supplies. Their self-absorption prevents recognition of their partners' needs and precludes giving back in equal measure.

When two self-important types are drawn to each other, it is not long before an emotional gulf develops between them. Although each expects the other to provide approbation, neither is willing to offer it.

After five years of marriage, Jan and Jonathan found themselves in this bleak situation. Originally attracted to each other by their similar natures, they soon learned that their alikeness also created problems. Both were demanding, egocentric, and competitive. Both made their careers top priority and were afraid of the other holding them back. When they were in open conflict —which was often —neither was able to see their partner's position. Each felt the other was selfish and uncaring.

> **Jan:** *The first few years of our marriage were a constant battle. We were at each other's throats. I think we were both disappointed in how little we got from each other. I know I was. I always expected my husband would give me respect and attention. Jonathan just didn't come through. He's too involved with his career and his image. He doesn't seem really interested in me. He resents my having needs, especially if they interfere with his plans. He wants me to take care of him, but he won't do the same for me.*

> **Jonathan:** *My biggest gripe with Jan is that she's too demanding. She's always asking for attention in one way or another. And when she doesn't get it, there's hell to pay. One time she was upset by a situation at work and I was preoccupied with something else. She made such a big stink about it, you'd think I had done something dreadful. I can't tell you the number of times she's ignored me when I needed her.*

Like many couples, Jan and Jonathan were quick to notice the other's problems and blind to the same processes in themselves. Each felt entitled to special treatment, yet neither was willing to provide it. Accustomed to being on the receiving end all their lives, the "giving" role was unfamiliar and unpracticed.

Extramarital Affairs: Convenient Narcissistic Supplies

Several years into their marriage, Jan began to feel depressed and developed intestinal problems. When she was alone, she experienced an intense feeling of hurt and disregard. She felt invalidated by her husband and turned to other relationships with friends and colleagues at work. But no one was able to supply the degree and intensity of attention she craved. She resolved the situation by having an affair with one of the young lawyers in her office. Although she considered him less than an equal in status and attractiveness, he was just what she needed: a man who would clearly see her uniqueness and appreciate her precisely because of it.

An extramarital tryst is nothing if not a source of narcissistic supplies. Its temporal, electric qualities are a bromide for feelings of low self-esteem and unattractiveness. So it was for Jan. She found herself more and more drawn to her lover, and her marriage, already badly strained, was stretched to a new dimension of aloofness. She spent longer periods away from Jonathan, ostensibly at her office.

Gradually her husband began to recognize something had changed. He suspected her of other involvements but had no information to support his intuition. Finally, one evening he overheard her on the phone with her lover. He was shocked. Despite their drifting from each other, he had never expected her to look for someone else. He felt hurt and in some curious way envious, but he hid both these emotions behind a facade of muted resentment. He pretended to be above the cool anger that brooded within him. In response, Jan was contrite. She felt guilty but did not regret seeking a companion who would gratify her needs. Yet the pressure of maintaining two relationships and the ever-growing realization that her lover was only a vehicle for her sexual desire took a toll on her. Several months later, she ended the liaison.

But Jonathan held onto his resentment. He would not forgive her. He experienced Jan's actions as demeaning, a slap in his face. He could not see her behavior as a function of her own needs. He perceived every event only in terms of its influence on him.

Months later, after time had cooled the intensity of his feelings and the two of them were again relating in their usual manner, he took up with another woman. The affair lasted only a few weeks and Jan never found out about it. Jonathan's motivation was complex. He acted partially out of revenge, but his primitive desire for retribution did not fully explain the whirlwind of emotions he felt in the pit of his stomach. Her affair had knocked him off his pedestal and reduced him to a cuckold. Haunted by the thought that he was just another sap, he sought a way to neutralize these feelings. The interest of another woman inflated his injured ego and restored his self-respect.

Early History: A Special Role

Jan was the oldest of two daughters in a well-to-do family. She grew up in a sheltered suburban community and attended local schools until she went off to a selective eastern women's college. As the first grandchild in her family, her birth was met with great anticipation. She was seen as an exceptional child, fussed over and indulged with every affection. Her mother was delighted with the commotion her daughter caused. She saw Jan's specialness as an appropriate reflection of herself

The first four years of Jan's life continued in this vein. No matter how commonplace her achievements, whatever she did was noted and praised. She was dressed up in pretty clothes, taught sophisticated stories and songs, and presented with countless gifts and toys so that her room resembled a toy store display before Christmas.

When she was four, the pattern changed. Her sister was born and her mother's attentions were directed elsewhere. The loss might have been traumatic had not another event occurred simultaneously. Her father was in a serious automobile accident, and his recovery required a long convalescence at home. This event provided Jan with an even better companion than her mother. Her father had little to do but observe his daughter, who delighted him with her precocious wit and charm. Jan became "Daddy's little girl" — his obvious favorite.

But as her father recovered and returned to work, she lost her captive and appreciative audience. Although she understood that he was compelled to earn a living, she felt hurt and abandoned by his abrupt departure, and deeply disappointed that her special relationship had been dissolved. Nevertheless, she maintained her favored role in the family. Admired and imitated by her younger sister and cousins, she did well in school and was doted on by her piano and ballet teachers. But the situation was not as ideal as it seemed. Although her parents did not interfere with her emerging sense of independence and gratified her material needs, their primary concern was how she reflected on them. Their attentiveness and praise were motivated not only by their love but by a personal investment in her actions and achievements. They saw her as a representation of themselves and their family, not as an individual unto herself.

As Jan matured, she recognized that the specialness she now craved and regarded as her right was highly conditional. When she did not perform well, her parents seemed less interested in her. Not that they chastised or admonished. They rewarded her achievements and dismissed her failures as aberrations. But as reasonable as their behavior seemed to them, it caused problems for her.

The truth of her situation was that her feelings of doubt, anxiety, and inadequacy — potential obstacles to her performance — were unacceptable and probably uncomfortable for her parents. They tried to extinguish them by acting as if they did not exist. But Jan needed to express her doubts and be assured that she was O.K. despite her imperfections. In fact, her mother's failure to accept her feelings of vulnerability left her wondering whether her parents would continue to love her if she were unsuccessful and reflected poorly on them.

To resolve her disappointment in their response and to meet their expectations for high performance, she learned to hold her anxieties in check through determination and stubborn self-control. She gave up trying to get acknowledgment of her feelings of inadequacy and became critical of them. She would not tolerate their expression. She became rigid and unyielding, her softer emotions buried and inaccessible. Her range of feeling was sacrificed for the sake of control. She rarely felt anxious but neither did she experience joy or exhilaration.

As she approached adulthood, armored against her own doubts and apprehensions, she found it harder to relax, slow down, and be receptive to the world around her. Her ability to maintain friendships suffered. She had difficulty feeling empathy and tenderness for those close to her. Her exaggerated sense of self-importance — cultivated by her family — reasserted itself along with the corollary belief that she deserved her special status. She saw herself as unique and superior, and her vanity required a diet of constant attention and favored treatment.

Jonathan's background was not so different from Jan's. He was the only son and oldest child in a middle-class family. Like Jan, he received a great deal of early attention and was clearly his parents' favorite. He was shown off to relatives and neighbors and treated like a prize. He had an especially close relationship with his mother which even his father seemed to envy. There was an adult flavor to their interaction. He was her "little man," and a mild sexual flirtation could be detected between them.

His parents maintained high expectations for him. They applauded his achievements at school, and were particularly proud of the fact that he assumed a leadership role among his peers. He was class president, editor of the school newspaper, and captain of the basketball team. On the occasions when he failed to do well, he felt painfully humiliated. For Jonathan, any flaw in performance was experienced as failure. He knew that his mother in particular would be disappointed. Unlike Jan's parents, she did not hesitate to criticize his failures. He wanted to avoid these unpleasant confrontations as well as maintain the pleasure of reporting his triumphs. Intuitively, he recognized that she was enormously invested in his success. Her undisguised scorn of those who were unsuccessful and her admiration of individuals who had distinguished themselves were relative constants in her conversations with him. He knew his mother felt a gain in stature as a result of his achievements. In fact, sometimes he thought that her expectations for him were designed to meet her wishes exclusively. In those moments he felt used.

Every child must contend with the dilemmas posed by parental expectations. For Jonathan, the pressures to be a "success" were much greater than, for example, the expectations that he be "moral," "artistic," or "sweet." The result was that by adolescence he had locked himself into a particular path and by early adulthood his own expectations for success exceeded even his mother's. This choice required determination and self-control. At college and graduate school, he studied hard and allowed few diversions. Most of his energy was devoted to work; his marriage and friendships played a comparatively minor role except as they supported his strivings.

He became increasingly absorbed in himself. He spent a great deal of time and effort on his personal appearance. His clothing, his hair style, and physical condition were important to him, and he was keenly aware of the image he projected although he took pains to appear casual about it. His bearing suggested pride and superiority, but there was also a hint of excessive constraint in it. He appeared bound by his own needs for control and performance.

Jan and Jonathan were two of a kind. Though the details of their histories differed, the patterns were remarkably similar. Both maintained a privileged position in their respective families, which directly influenced their inflated sense of self-importance. Each was the recipient of abundant material gratification, evoking feelings of entitlement. Both experienced high expectations for achievement and a loss of parental approval when they failed, a situation which led them to equate performance with personal worth. And each had a strong relationship with the opposite-sex parent that fed their motivation to meet parental expectations.

Misguided Astronomers

Self-important individuals are engrossed in themselves. They like nothing more than to talk about the details of their lives, regardless of how mundane, and they seem to think that others are equally interested. They are poor listeners who often redirect the subject of discussion back to their own exploits. They are frequently exhibitionistic in an attempt to gain attention and praise.

Some are drawn to intensive psychotherapy by the constant failure of their relationships, but many come simply to gain the fixed regard of another human being. What could be more satisfying than sitting with an individual whose sole function is to listen and sort through the principal experiences of one's life? That much scrutiny is a covert affirmation of specialness. No wonder self-important individuals are found in large numbers among the "experience junkies" who try every new psychological technique in the name of personal growth. Most are there not to change for the better but to feed their egocentricity. They crave the focus on self for its own sake.

Like misguided astronomers, self-important types believe the universe revolves around their personal planet. To shift their frame of reference from "me" to "you" requires maximum effort. In couple therapy, for example, they usually have problems with the "role reversal" exercise in which each partner takes the other's viewpoint. They are too self-engrossed to recognize another's perspective, and they are quick to classify as foes those who do not support their position.

Disappointment and the Self-Important Style

The self-important style leads inevitably to chronic disappointment because it is based on exaggerated assumptions about one's self that society is expected to mirror. An inflated sense of personal worth produces expectations that are grandiose. Self-important individuals often believe they can succeed where others have failed, that nothing can stop them from achieving their goals, and that they will always get what they want. But there is one underlying expectation: the belief that they are *entitled* to privileged treatment without earning it. This idea crudely translates to "I expect to get what I want because I want it!" Such a pretentious attitude is a far cry from the humble thoughts of the "deprived" individual. Self-important types represent the other extreme. They are convinced their specialness justifies a positive response to their request for a bank loan, college application, or marriage proposal. Inevitably, they are let down when their overblown wishes are shattered by reality or when society fails to recognize their claims.

Relationships, however, are where their greatest disappointments occur. These individuals see intimacy as an arena in which to gain admiration and attention. They exploit it for their own ends, usually without success. One of two scenarios generally occurs:

- The partner, feeling used, refuses to provide any more approbation, and ends the relationship.

- The self-important individual disparages both the partner and quality of attention received. He or she withdraws emotional investment and looks for another to provide satisfaction.

Intimacy requires surrendering to feeling and transcending one's own boundaries. It means yielding to a larger purpose, a union greater than the self. And it demands giving for its own pleasure without concern for what is to be gained. Consumed by their needs for achievement, self-control, and constant attention, these people do poorly at love. And because love is received in proportion to one's capacity to give it, in the end their greatest disappointment is their inability to receive the love they crave.

The self-important style, characterized by grandiose expectations, is based on the lifewish to be special. To surrender that illusory desire, these individuals must accept their ordinariness and develop a more balanced picture of themselves. It is not an easy solution. For them, ordinary means worthless. I remember the words of one of my patients who remarked despairingly, "To see myself as an average person like everyone else would destroy me." But recognizing the characteristics of all humanity in oneself enlarges rather than shrinks the self. Every one of us is a combination of common and special qualities. We

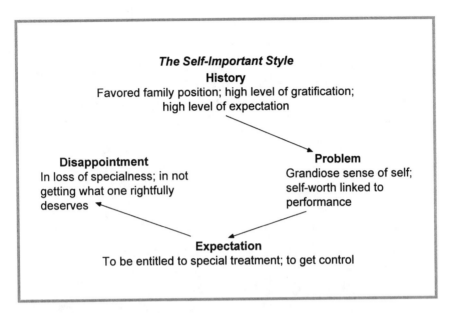

The Self-Important Style
History
Favored family position; high level of gratification;
high level of expectation

Disappointment
In loss of specialness; in not
getting what one rightfully
deserves

Problem
Grandiose sense of self;
self-worth linked to
performance

Expectation
To be entitled to special treatment; to get control

are capable of both greatness and mediocrity. Even Einstein acknowledged he was a lousy driver. Those who see themselves as greater than others are seeing only half the picture.

Before indulging in aggrandizement, the self-important individual would do well to take a closer look at the limitations of the human condition. For all our diverseness and productivity, we have yet to answer the most fundamental questions: "Why do we live?" and "What follows life?" And despite the combined knowledge of generations, we have not found a means to eradicate violence and war. We are a highly fallible and corruptible species, of questionable significance in the larger scheme of the universe. When we consider that our sun is only one star among a hundred billion others in this galaxy alone, and that there are numberless other galaxies, the shallowness of our daily concerns is inescapable. This perspective dwarfs the grandiosity of self-important individuals and renders it absurd.

Chapter 9

Expectation: The Key to Preventing Disappointment

Nothing is as good as it seems beforehand.
— George Eliot

The quality of our expectations determines the quality of our actions.
— Andre Grodin

Expectation is a puzzling phenomenon. It has the capacity to both enlarge and diminish our experience. It can inspire us to superhuman feats beyond the realm of scientific knowledge, or it can severely limit our lives to the commonplace. It can heal the sick and give heart to the hopeless, but it may just as easily distract our perceptions and dull our awareness.

The influence of expectation is seen in daily events. One patient is given medication for an illness. Another takes a sugar pill, assuming it to be a potent drug. Both recover with equal speed. The expectation that the sugar pill will be therapeutic produces the cure. Indeed, placebos are acknowledged to be effective in 20-40 percent of medical cases.

The influence of expectation on healing is age-old. In primitive cultures, local shamans often traded on faith and strong conviction, masquerading both beneath potions and symbols. What really cured was the unshakeable and absolute belief in the power of the magic. Conversely, belief in the negative symbol could have harmful effects. Walter Cannon of Harvard reported numerous cases of individuals who died only hours after a voodoo shaman put the curse on them. In the right context, expectation can produce extraordinary results.

But expectation has other less miraculous functions. It is helpful in planning for the future and eliminating surprise. It projects us into the next day or year so we are able to foresee what is required and respond accordingly. It provides a mental dress rehearsal of sorts which allows us to prepare for a variety of contingencies. Particularly in matters of security and survival, this is a matchless ability which to some extent explains our survival as a species. To a lesser degree, activities such as retirement planning, buying a smoke alarm, or saving money for our child's education demonstrate the value of expectation in preparing for the long haul.

Expectation also organizes our view of the world. We perceive in accordance with what we expect to see. This is because our anticipations set a context for how we will process new information. A photograph of a house cat inadvertently introduced by the photographer as a picture of a mountain lion will probably be interpreted in line with the viewer's expectation. Likewise, a vague shadow in a darkened room may be seen as a menacing figure if we are feeling fearful or vulnerable.

We see an extreme form of expectation's grip on perception in the individual with a paranoid disorder. He moves through life with the persistent and continued expectation that someone or something is out to get him. If offered food, he may think it poisoned. If given shelter, he may expect the room to be bugged. A pedestrian who looks askance at his odd behavior is judged as malevolent and a further sign of the conspiracy against him. All events are organized according to the delusional anticipation that the world will be hostile to him. To some extent the expectation is self-fulfilling, since his actions arouse discomfort and antipathy in others. But his continued madness is insured primarily by the flawed arrangement of his perceptions.

The Love Affair with Expectation

"And what wine is so sparkling, what so fragrant, what so intoxicating, as possibility?" The Danish philosopher Kierkegaard wrote these words 150 years ago to describe the love affair human beings carry on with expectation. We love to "look forward to." We love to contemplate tomorrow. Sometimes we miss sleep thinking about the events of the next day. Other times we fantasize about the coming reunion with old friends or our rendezvous with a new lover. We relish expectation because thinking about events brings them to present consciousness and gives us a delightful taste of what is to come. Expectation builds excitement. We commonly use it to raise the level of desire. It is the force that transforms ordinary wish into yearning. In this sense it exists in the service of passion, a special form of aphrodisiac, concocted by the imagination of possibility. Consider these examples:

> *A young child is going to the circus for the first time. Her mind races with the thoughts and images she has associated with the Big Top. She contemplates coming face to face with lions and tigers, clowns and trapeze artists. She replays these images in her mind until she can barely contain her excitement.*

A studious eighteen-year-old is preparing for her first year of college. She daydreams about living on her own, the stimulating classes, and the formation of new friendships. She particularly enjoys imagining literature courses where she sees herself in a dialogue with her erudite professors discussing Dostoevsky, Shakespeare and Blake. Anticipation of these exchanges creates feelings of pure delight. She experiences herself as very adult and wise.

A former college athlete has joined a weekend softball team. Although she has not played in fifteen years, in her mind she pictures herself moving with grace and skill as she fields ground balls and picks off line drives. She envisions hitting home runs and trotting around the bases to the cheers of the crowd. She meditates on these glorious expectations, increasing her desire to get out and play.

In each situation, imagining possibility builds excitement and generates energy. The child, student, and former athlete draw on past experience, association, and fantasy to create a thought picture of what is to come. These images — whether fact or fancy — stimulate desire and send a tremor of exhilaration through the mind and body. They create aliveness and stir the blood. They sharpen the senses and increase delight with the future. Samuel Johnson said it well: "We love to expect, and when expectation is either disappointed or gratified, we want to be again expecting."

Negative Expectation

There are really two kinds of expectation: positive and negative, each reflecting how we envision what is to come. On the one hand, positive expectation results in disappointment when it goes unmet. On the other, failed negative expectation brings relief and sometimes unbridled joy.

All positive expectation contains an assessment and a wish for a certain course of events. "I expect to have a good time" means "I want to" and "In all probability I will." Negative expectation contains an assessment and a fear. "I expect she won't love me" equals "In all likelihood she won't" and "I'm afraid she won't." Negative expectations are always defensive in character. Historically, our first expectations are exclusively positive, strongly embodying our wishes. But as we grow up and in the process experience disappointment, we develop negative expectations, mostly as a way to protect ourselves from being let down. "I expect she won't love me" is really a maneuver to protect against failure of the wish "I want her to love me."

Negative expectations mirror our fears, especially those dreaded thoughts that our wishes will go ungratified. We will measure the effectiveness of this sort of disappointment defense later in the chapter.

The Other Side of the Story

The very aspects of expectation that benefit us also work to our disadvantage. When we anticipate an event, we create a mental set on the future, That is, we program our minds to notice only the things we expect to see. In doing so, we limit what we can take in. Our expectation acts as a kind of screen to other stimuli. An old Yiddish folktale demonstrates this point.

A seeker travels hundreds of miles on foot through natural and man-made adversity to learn the mysteries of life from a renowned tsaddik. After much misadventure he arrives exhausted in the tiny village and inquires where he can find the famous sage whose reputation is known far and wide. Given directions, he proceeds to a small hovel where he encounters an old man dressed in rags, as unkempt as a beggar and obviously very poor.

Startled that a man of such wisdom could appear so wretched but not wishing to offend him, the seeker introduces himself, identifies his mission, and sits down. The old man immediately sets before him a meal of wine and cheese.

The seeker, still disturbed by the old man's appearance and living conditions, can barely contain himself and blurts out, "How can such a thing be? I did not expect this at all!"

To which the sage calmly replies, "What, you were expecting maybe herring with sour cream?"

The seeker expected someone grander and more pretentious than the figure in rags standing before him. He has trouble adjusting to the new circumstances. The sage, at ease with himself, chooses not to acknowledge the man's disappointment in his appearance. Instead, he trivializes the man's reaction. It is as if he were saying, "What you expected me to look like is of no consequence. Don't let your lost expectation deter you from your real mission!"

Expectations — met or unmet — draw our attention away from other, sometimes more important perceptions. We have the capacity to be so engrossed in our anticipations that, like the seeker, we are distracted from what is in front of our nose. Expecting to see an airplane in the night sky, we miss the shooting star or, for that matter, don't notice that someone is picking our pocket. Expectation has the power to limit as well as enhance the experience. A male friend, a teacher in his early thirties, struggled for a number of years over whether to marry a particular woman. In many ways, she was a wonderful life partner for him. They shared mutual interests, enjoyed each other's company, dealt well with conflict, loved and respected one another. My friend was troubled, however, by this woman's past. She had been a topless dancer for a brief period in her life, and with his strict religious background he would not tolerate this one flaw. He expected the woman he married to be as pure as Sierra snow, and his continued focus on this minor aspect of her past distracted him from the sensational woman she in fact was. His expectation — and his subsequent disappointment in her — limited his vision. He could only see the imperfections in the diamond. The beauty and luster were lost to him.

As we already know, expecting helps to eliminate the threat or discomfort associated with surprise. Anticipation can be thought of as mental preparation, and we can hardly be startled if we are prepared. But the cost of living with a future that is predictable can be exorbitant. When all events are anticipated, we lose our sense of adventure. We do not permit life to unfold before us, or respond to events as they come. As much as expectation may increase excitement, it also has the equal facility to make things too safe, too predictable. Boredom and caution travel the same road.

For all its advantage, expectation can feel like a burden. When we hold impossibly high standards for our behavior, we create the preconditions for disappointment in self. More than that, we make life ponderous and exhausting, since we are always trying to live up to a level of perfection that is unattainable. Some people believe that without high expectations they would be slothful or indolent. They assume the only thing that keeps them on track is their internal requirement for excellence. Such people are genuinely unhappy because they are unwilling to accept themselves for all that they are — good and bad, outstanding and mediocre.

Likewise, when we assume an obligation to fulfill the expectations of important people around us — our spouses, parents, teachers — we generally feel encumbered. We do it in order to win their favor, avoid disapproval, and gain increased self-esteem. But attending to the real or imagined agenda of others creates a situation in which we lose sight of our own desires and needs. Our sense of identity is never allowed full expression, and eventually we're left resentfully seeking a way to live expectation-free.

Clearly, expectations can be helpful allies or dreaded foes. A great deal depends on how deeply we invest in them and how much we identify them with ourselves. If we look at the current popular notions regarding expectation, three approaches stand out. Each offers a flawed remedy for the elimination of disappointment.

The All-Positive Approach

This notion is rooted in the one-sided view that if we expect good things for ourselves — indeed, envision them actively — they will come to pass. Credo: "Imagine it and it will happen." Such thinking suggests that expectation psychologically prepares the individual for success and eliminates negative self-fulfilling ideas. The formula runs something like this: If you expect to be successful, think and act successfully; eventually you'll arrive at the wished-for destination. There is some truth in this proposition. Believing in yourself and setting your sights on what you want can have salutary effects. The athlete who does not believe he will win the race is less likely to do so. The sales executive who is certain she will close the deal is more apt to accomplish the feat than a doubting competitor.

As an overall approach to expectation, however, this will-driven view is incomplete and misleading. For one thing, it offers no qualifications and no limits, implying that expecting anything long and hard enough will produce the desired result. This is nothing more than wishful thinking presented in the guise of popular wisdom. Believing in fairies won't keep Tinker Bell alive no matter how committed you are to the idea.

Once, when I stated this position on the radio, an incredulous talk show host chided me: "What about the great woman track star who was paralyzed by polio as a child? If she hadn't dreamt of running in the Olympics, she'd never have won that gold medal." I've no doubt this is true. People with extreme physical disabilities and life-threatening disease need hope to maintain their will to construct a livable future. Sometimes that hope makes all the difference. But these are exceptional cases where a dream may be about the only thing left to hang onto. In less extreme situations, dreams must be tempered by the rules of reality. Expect true love to solve all problems, every prayer to be answered, life to be fair or free of pain and disease, and you're surely setting yourself up for disappointment. A track star may dream she will one day run at the Olympics but if she imagines she'll run the mile in under two minutes that's another thing entirely. It is important to dream but equally important to stay within the bounds of possibility.

Research on high achieving individuals shows that one of the characteristics distinguishing them from their less successful counterparts is that they don't bite off more than they can chew. They set realistic goals. They may dream but their everyday behavior reflects a more practical assessment of what they can accomplish. And they are always modifying their goals as the situation changes. They solicit and read feedback continuously so they know if they're on target. The hallmark of these individuals is flexibility and vigilance.

One of my patients described an experience he had while mountain biking. If he focused his attention on the top of the long, steep hill he felt discouraged and lost energy. But if he kept his focus on the area about twenty yards ahead of him he pedaled with vigor. Why? Sometimes dreams and expectations motivate, sometimes they enervate if the task seems too overwhelming. We need to aspire but to heights just outside our grasp, heights that stretch but do not strain us.

The thought that anything can be accomplished with enough will or commitment is soft-headed and a reflection of a culture that doesn't want to accept any limits. Such a wildly optimistic view cannot help but attract us. Yet it denies the real character of existence with its pleasure and pain, despair as well as joy. No one is immune from the "slings and arrows of outrageous fortune." Writer-philosopher Sam Keen writes convincingly:

> *Life is not a bowl of Librium. And a good part of the secret of happiness lies in learning to suffer with dignity. Loneliness, loss, disappointment, failure, disease, boredom are inevitable. The price of trying to avoid the unavoidable is illusion, or neurosis. Even if you jog, eat health foods, grow, meditate, and go to confession regularly you will sometimes fall sick... Your best-laid plans won't coerce the future. Nothing you can do will keep those you love from dying. You can never be fully safe. The fears of abandonment and annihilation are in the DNA. They are the Siamese twin of the will to live.*

The Doomsday Approach

This rather cynical viewpoint assumes that expecting the worst is a sure-fire antidote for disappointment. Credo: "Only fools are satisfied." The approach represents a 180-degree shift from the all-positive position. It relies exclusively on negative expectation. If things work out better than anticipated, so much the better. Such an outlook is distinctly defensive and is worse than the condition it purports to cure. One does not expect a routine surgery to fail as preparation for that possibility. Doing so only creates unnecessary worry and stress.

Individuals who have previously suffered deep disappointment are most likely to subscribe to this kind of twisted defense as insurance against future letdown. The illogic and underlying despair contained within it is rarely admitted. Indeed the proponents of this viewpoint are frequently cheerleaders for cynicism, passionate and unmovable in their commitment to the negative outcome. Expecting the worst eliminates disappointment by symptom substitution. It creates pessimism and gloom masquerading as worldliness.

Just as positive expectations can be self-fulfilling, so too are negative expectations. People who expect unpleasantness set themselves up through their negativity to receive it. Like flypaper to the fly, they seem to attract calamity. The ballplayer who expects to drop the fly ball usually fails to make the catch. The job hunter who expects to do poorly on the interview most often does. Negative expectation can create negative experience which, in turn, reinforces the belief that low expectation is justifiable. And so the doomsday cycle is perpetuated.

Sometimes negative expectation *is* justifiable and realistic. Patients I have seen, for example, have been reared by toxic parents who have severe emotional problems and are incapable of loving them or even responding to them with civility. In such circumstances, the negative expectation, "I won't get what I want from my mother," is entirely appropriate and, in fact, a correct assessment of reality. But every situation does not require a negative appraisal. As an approach to expectation, the doomsday notion is highly unsuccessful because it helps create the very situation of disappointment it is attempting to combat.

The Eradication Approach

This view would have us live without expectation. By anticipating nothing and accepting events as they come, disappointment would be eliminated. Credo: "Be here now." There is merit in the idea of present-centeredness, of living in the here and now without preconceived notions of what we want from the future. All the problems caused by expectation would be eliminated if we could rid ourselves of the expectation habit. But can we? And what do we lose in the process?

We lose a great deal. The capacity to expect adds a richness to our lives that cannot be overlooked or discounted. Without it, we reduce the level of excitation and passion, forego planning and organizing functions, lessen our motivation and with it our hopes for the future. The forfeit of expectation results in an impoverishment of our lives that can only be compared to the sacrifice of imagination or the ability to dream great dreams. Those who advocate the eradication of expectation are sometimes the same individuals who have suffered such serious disappointment that they are afraid of ever wanting anything strongly again. One of my patients was a dancer who, after years of preparing for her career, suffered an injury to her knee that left her unable to continue. Her disappointment was monumental. She saw her whole life as preparation for a journey that was now impossible to take. Dismayed and despairing, she defended against similar circumstances by not allowing herself any intense desire. She became blase and indifferent, almost frozen in her rigid defense. Only by risking "wanting" again was she able to overcome her despair.

Even if we are willing to eliminate expectation, the question remains as to whether human beings are capable of such an adjustment over the long haul. Perhaps in the confines of a time-limited vacation, a protected environment, or in a defensive paralysis, yes, but it is unrealistic to believe that in modern life — with all its stress and complexity — we can live without expectations. It would require superhuman discipline and energy, and a level of perfection that is uncharacteristic of the species. The eradication approach is really a utopian vision of life without general applicability to large numbers of people. The best that we can hope for is a reduction in the level of expectation. Elimination is virtually impossible. Like fear of abandonment or annihilation, it is built into the DNA.

Preventing Chronic Disappointment

It is always a dangerous business to advocate a particular psychological solution to a problem as universal and recurrent as disappointment. To do so is to oversimplify the issues involved and risk excluding those whose unique situations do not seem relevant. Worse, there is the danger of setting up unrealistic expectations. We already know the consequences of that action.

With these concerns in mind, I am putting forth six basic principles which, sensibly followed, will reduce chronic disappointment. I do not say "eliminate," for that task is truly impossible. In life, disappointment is inevitable and also of value in shaping our world view and helping us to fathom possibility. (More on this in Chapter 11.)

Two notions are essential to our task. First, the attitude we hold toward expectation is critical. Second, the degree of realism reflected in our expectations determines whether they succeed or fail, and hence how disappointed we are.

Six Principles

Flexible Attitude

The first step in forming a new relationship with expectation is to maintain a more flexible attitude. Keep perspective on your expectations. Be prepared to change them when circumstances indicate they're unlikely to be met. Don't invest too heavily in any one outcome.

Keep Perspective: Approach expectations without reverence or attachment. No expectations are sacrosanct. Few involve matters of life and death. And none are irreplaceable. As important as expectation in general may be in helping us to function in the world, no single hoped-for outcome is essential. Remember that expectations are nothing more than wish and anticipation. Don't empower them with the twin illusions of necessity or indispensability. Don't give them royal treatment or see them as permanent fixtures that cannot be removed or changed without great pain. Think of them as dessert, delicious and tempting but not obligatory. Expectations are helpful and pleasurable only if we see them clearly without overvaluing them.

Be Prepared to Change: A key to reducing disappointment is a willingness to give up what you want when you can't get it. Consider the situation of the first time homebuyer who goes into the marketplace with a Beverly Hills wish list and a Costco budget. Without a willingness to surrender expectations this situation is not going to end happily. Or the tourist who finds the hotel lost his reservation and he's going to have to spend the night in that seedy fleabag down the block. Those who are able to adjust to the contingencies of unexpected circumstances rarely feel disappointed.

Reduce Your Investment: Some people overly invest in their expectations. As a result, they hold onto them long after it is advisable, suffering disappointment in the process. We need to reduce and sometimes liquidate our investments. The problem is both in the degree of attachment we feel to our particular desires and in the intensity of our wants. "But I was really looking forward to having a steak," a friend bellyached at a favorite restaurant one night. When the waiter suggested the fish instead he pouted like a little boy who's just learned the trip to Disneyland's been cancelled. In our culture where so many have so much, we take our wants very seriously and precisely. We don't just want a car, but a specific model in a particular color with a definite set of features. We want choices, we want service, we want convenience, we want it all. And we expect to get it or come close. No wonder we have problems maintaining flexible desires.

We've come to identify with our expectations as if they were a measure of ourselves. The woman who hopes to rise one day to the top of the corporate hierarchy would look unfavorably on relinquishing that dream. Perhaps she relies on it for motivation, but it's a pretty good guess she sees it as self-defining. Dreaming great dreams reflects well on the dreamer. And if she cannot achieve her expectation, she can at least separate herself from the herd by anticipating a wondrous future.

Although we may enjoy associating ourselves with great expectations, what we *do* in reality is a far better criterion of individual merit than what we expect. Even the ne'er-do-well may envision a life of fame and fortune. In identifying with our expectations, we give them an authority and urgency which they do not truly deserve. To maintain an elastic attitude we need to remember that we are not our expectations. They do not define us any more than does our shoe size.

Trim Down Expectations

We expect too much! In a culture where we feel we *deserve* to be gratified, most of us expect a great deal from life, particularly in the important areas of sex, relationship, work, and family. With the breakdown of familiar sex roles it is not uncommon to expect one's spouse to be all things from lover to business partner. The burden of such expectations is a significant load to bear. No one's shoulders are wide enough, and many relationships fail as a consequence of the disappointment and resentment that necessarily follow. Likewise, we expect a great deal more from our jobs than previous generations. We are working longer hours, and consequently the workplace is expected to fulfill many social needs previously met in our private lives. With the death of company loyalty as a corporate ideal many employees will be further disappointed. In the age of Aids, sex has changed too. Except among teenagers promiscuity has diminished, although pity the lover who is not sensitive, nurturing, exciting, communicative, willing, and sexually knowledgeable. Surely we have set the stage for disillusionment among the actors in this drama.

To prevent disappointment, we must reduce the sheer number of expectations that we hold and scale them down to meet the realities of current life. Perhaps Andre Gide was right when he said, "Long only for what you have." But no one wants to hear this sort of message. Many a politician has been forced into early retirement for advocating that we lower our expectations to reflect greater realism.

The deeper psychological truth is that our desires are often confused and poorly conceived. Not knowing what will truly bring us happiness, we entertain all sorts of desires in the hope of finding that one object or situation that will bring satisfaction. We operate under the misconception that fulfillment of large numbers of wants and expectations is correlated with happiness. The fulfillment of a dozen meaningless desires, however, merely results in more disappointment and confusion when we feel no better: "Why don't these things make me happy?" In the end we ask, "Is that all there is?"

Choose your dreams carefully. Sometimes we pursue what we "should" or "ought to," not what is genuinely satisfying or fitting. Other times we hold expectations for ourselves which are either impossible to attain or simply unsuited to our level of skill and ability. We would like to be a distinguished professor, a professional athlete, an internationally-known opera star, but are our talents and natural endowments equal to the task?

To avoid disappointment in self, our expectations should be realistic and based on a practical assessment of our capabilities. Know what you can do and pursue it. Expect of yourself only what you are capable of achieving and what you really want. What expectations are yours by conscious choice as opposed to those learned automatically at your parent's knee? When expectations are trimmed down to a manageable number and grounded in honest assessments of capability, the preconditions for disappointment are reduced.

Use More Assessment, Less Wish

Another way of preventing disappointment is to change the nature of expectations. As I noted earlier, every desired expectation combines both a wish and an assessment of possibility. "I expect to get the job" means both "I am looking forward to being hired" and "I will likely be hired." When the relationship between these components is askew, we create the preconditions for letdown. Chronically disappointed individuals not only fail to develop realistic expectations, they also put too much wish and too little assessment in what they anticipate will happen. Overly influenced by desire and not heedful of probability they respond like young children who have not yet developed a sense of realism. Consequently, their expectations often fail.

Consider the state lotteries. Americans spend billions of dollars each year to purchase these little tickets with the big payoffs. "Someone's got to win so why not me?" is the conventional wisdom. But do you actually expect to cash in? Are you planning your retirement based on hoped-for lottery revenues? Of course not. It's an extremely low probability situation and that's exactly how we should approach it when our ticket doesn't pay off. A university statistician once remarked that the probability of winning is so low that the lottery should be seen as a form of entertainment not as an investment strategy. Yet it's this sort of lottery thinking that is usually behind many disappointments. People want the world to be fair, the bad to be punished, the good guys to win and so forth. Their expectations reflect it.

The remedy is not rocket science or magic. Put more assessment into expectations and take out the wish component. This strategy requires something uncommon: clarity about what you expect to happen. That doesn't sound like much to ask, but I am always surprised how unconscious people can be when it comes to something as commonplace as expectations. "Hadn't really thought about it" is a response I often get to questions about what people expect in situations like a trip back home to see the folks or a college reunion. Once you get clear on what you expect to happen you can assess the likelihood that it will. Ask not only, "Is it possible?" but also, "Is it possible in this particular situation?" Probability cannot be measured without consideration of context. Finding a partner to create family may be a realistic goal. Finding that person in an nursing is not.

Eliminate Absolute and Exacting Expectations

Perfectionists — people with exacting expectations for themselves and others — usually suffer a great deal more disappointment than others. But they are not the only ones with precise requirements for satisfaction. Many of us hold expectations so demanding or absolute that their fulfillment is virtually impossible to achieve. It's not uncommon for spouses to expect their partners to be cheerful and attentive on arriving home or for someone to believe her life should be a model of productivity and efficiency or her friends to be available whenever they're needed. At first glance, none of these presumptions seems patently unreasonable because we assume that an occasional slipup will be tolerated, chalked up to human fallibility. However, when expectations are burdened with symbolism or the person holding them requires one hundred percent compliance, trouble can be expected.

The chronically disappointed tend to formulate absolute expectations. They use words such as "always," "never," and "every." Others, despite the qualified language of their expectations, act as if they were indeed absolute. "I expect you to be home most of the time" may imply, "I expect you to be home all the time." Since human beings are fallible, those who demand faultlessness are usually disappointed. "Why can't people act as responsibly as I do?" is their usual refrain. They operate under the misconception that absolute expectations bring out the best in themselves and others. Social research indicates this thinking is erroneous. Setting rigidly high standards rarely results in optimal performance, and most people react to the burden of impossible expectations with resentment.

Consider your own expectations. Are they absolute and overly demanding? Do you always expect your children to reflect well on you, or that every sexual experience be wonderfully satisfying? To prevent disappointment, we need to eliminate unconditional and peremptory expectations and substitute less narrow and more tolerant requirements for satisfaction. Take my friend Bob. He's the kind of person who seems to relish whatever he's doing. Once we planned a bicycle tour through Europe together. We spent more than a few weekends researching the trip at the local mega bookstore, but just as we were about to leave an airline strike sabotaged our plans and we had to cancel the whole enterprise. Was Bob disappointed? Did he mope around and curse his unlucky stars like I was doing? Not Bob. He was his usual chipper self.

"How do you do it?" I asked incredulously.

"Do what? We'll plan something else and have just as good a time, maybe even better. The important thing is to have an adventure. It doesn't matter where we go."

Bob's strategy works. He keeps his expectations flexible and general. That way, if a desired outcome fails there's no trauma or teeth gnashing. Just make a new plan. The important thing is "to go on an adventure." Expectations that are broad and loosely constructed are easier to satisfy and easier to tolerate if they are not fulfilled. Rigid and exacting expectations produce the opposite effect. They make gratification that much more difficult. The less absolute the expectation, the greater its chance for success.

Expect Some Disappointment

It is important to remember that some disappointment is going to occur no matter how judicious you may be. Provide for this possibility in your life so that you are prepared for occasional letdown. Such precaution is not the same as adopting negative expectations. It acknowledges the capricious nature of disappointment and the lack of certainty in daily living. There is no fail-safe method for preventing disappointment. The wish to eradicate it completely like a troublesome household pest is yet another unrealistic expectation that produces the very condition it purports to avoid.

Maintain Hope

As we pare down our expectations, eliminating the unnecessary, unrealistic, and absolute, we may find ourselves wondering how we will face tomorrow without the lifewishes and dreams that underlie our expectancies. What is the consequence of starting a relationship without any preconceptions, or interviewing for a job without an overriding attachment to getting it? We cannot know with certainty until we experiment with this new perspective.

In reducing expectations, we are eliminating particular wishes and dreams, but we do not have to discard the attitude of hope along with them. We can maintain it without investing in specific hopes. Hope, in the singular, is an outlook, a perspective on the future that cannot be destroyed by a single loss. It is larger than our attachments. Lifewishes may come and go but hope remains a statement that we believe in tomorrow. Chronic disappointment is the natural enemy of hope. The repeated experience of expecting and not receiving wears us down emotionally, erodes our optimism, and depletes our trust that circumstances will ever improve.

Ultimately, to live without habitual disappointment we must give up specific hopes but not the attitude of hoping. We must keep a vision of possibility without expecting it. Thus we look forward to the future, but we keep our expectations for new relationship, job, or vacation, as close to zero as possible. This requires from each of us a certain amount of mental discipline and an element of faith that life will turn out all right even if events do not go as we expected.

Chapter 10

Up from Disappointment

The greatest discovery of any generation is that human beings can alter their lives by altering their attitudes of mind.

— Albert Schweitzer

Although few people want to experience disappointment, many are fascinated by it. Literature abounds with classic stories of disappointed dreams and unrealized hopes. From Madame Bovary to Anna Karenina, Hamlet to Heathcliff, the drawing rooms, bedchambers, and misty moors of countless dramas hang heavy with despair and rude awakenings. None of those works is more graphic than the contemporary play, *Death of a Salesman.* In it, playwright Arthur Miller exposes the power of disappointment to undermine, corrupt, and finally destroy the lives of an American family. It is a tragic portrait of the common man, one Willy Loman, salesman, father, and husband, disillusioned with life and himself but unable to face his failures. To escape his disappointment, he mythologizes his success. But his talk is idle crowing. Willy has struggled all his life just to make ends meet. He is still a salesman after so many years, still driving the same lonely roads, selling undistinguished goods.

Recognizing his failures and changing his future is not in Willy's character. To escape the nagging truth, he directs his disappointment away from himself and onto his oldest son. Biff, a "golden boy" during childhood, has — like his father — failed to live up to the expected promise. At thirty-four he is still in search of himself, confused and unhappy. Contemptuous of his father, whom he had idolized until a traumatic incident in adolescence, he is impatient with Willy's self-deception. Ultimately these emotions poison the entire Loman family and force Willy into a desperate act of self-justification: He takes his own life so that his family will receive money from his insurance policy.

Death of a Salesman is a story about the ravages of disappointment. Willy hides from his dashed expectations by denying their failure. To the end, he is a man who misses the obvious. His wishes blur his vision and inevitably ruin him. Dreams are the last refuge of the disappointed, but the price of living through them is high. As the philosopher Thomas Hobbes reminds us, "Men are sometimes free to do what they wish, but they are never free in their wishes."

There are many lessons contained in this tragedy. One message is fundamental: The denial of disappointment is the gravest of errors. It leads us to a far greater desperation in the long run and prevents us from addressing the unrealistic expectations on which our feelings are based. Willy pretended he had made it big. Everyone else recognized his charade but chose to protect him from himself. They colluded in the deceit which eventually brought the man down.

Moving out of disappointment begins with a recognition of one's feelings of loss. This is step one. We cannot hope for improvement without acknowledging our dilemma and our need to change. Like Willy Loman, a surprisingly large number of individuals block awareness of their disappointment. They feel vague signs of distress: a depressive malaise, a loss of excitement, a nagging sense of defeat. But they don't attach these signals to any particular cause. Perhaps they are avoiding the self-evident, hoping it will go away like a sudden stomach pain or a pang of self-doubt. Maybe they see it as a Pandora's box that, once opened, will cause overwhelming problems. In opinion polls, which base their findings entirely on self-report, respondents tend to express high rates of personal satisfaction for themselves, but perceive lower rates for others. In a classic survey on the family, for example, seventy-six percent of those polled believed family life in America was in trouble, while eighty-five percent of the same group reported that most of their expectations of happiness in marriage had been fulfilled.

Can it be that we just don't like to admit to our own problems although we can easily detect them in our neighbors? Or are we projecting our troubles onto others while refusing to own up to them ourselves? Becoming aware of our difficulties forces us to decide whether to exert effort to change and possibly risk greater hazards or to do nothing and passively accept the current undesirable circumstances. By keeping up the illusion of happiness or projecting dissatisfaction onto others, we avoid consciousness of this unwelcome choice.

Why would anyone put off changing dysfunctional patterns that bring constant disappointment? Most people don't relish personal change. They're afraid of it. It makes them feel worried and anxious. But it's more complicated than that. Below are a few of the most popular explanations for why people resist change:

Every change involves contending with the unknown. The unknown is highly unpredictable and, therefore, filled with apprehension. The imagination's capacity to run wild upon entering a dark, unfamiliar room gives us some idea of how we can project catastrophic expectations onto new situations.

Change creates loss.   When we initiate a new course of action, we terminate at the same moment the old way of doing things. If we alter the way we relate to the boss, we discontinue the prior pattern of interaction. If we change an attitude or viewpoint, we surrender a former perspective — every change necessarily produces the loss of the status quo and that can be frightening. Unfortunately, relinquishing established patterns is a prerequisite for any alteration in the way things are.

Situations in which what is given up is valued less than what is gained present the easiest transitions. Few people have difficulty adjusting to color television after black and white. Circumstances in which what is lost is more attractive than what is gained discourage change. No one likes to think they are trading down.

Decision limits possibility.   By choosing A, we exclude B, C, and D. Each choice represents a number of paths rejected. Given the opportunity, who would not prefer to have unlimited options? Possibility is endless as long as we don't act. Exclusion begins as soon as we choose one change over another.

Change requires energy and commitment.   Those who live stressful lives do not relish additional pressure — and we all live stressful lives. Most of us have our hands full keeping all those balls in the air without introducing the effort required to change our expectations and habits. But what makes us think that life will be easier if we maintain the status quo? Positive personal growth allows us to deal more effectively with the world by eliminating self-defeating and repetitive neurotic patterns. Ask anyone who has ever conquered a phobia whether they are better off for having made the decision to challenge their anxieties.

Significant change often produces identity confusion. How we view ourselves is supported by the life roles we play in work and relationships, as well as by our daily rituals and familiar surroundings. Our sense of identity is buttressed by the milieu in which we live. Take away this context and the individual can feel as disoriented as the proverbial fish out of water. I knew a CEO who was much admired and respected in his industry. A decision in midlife to change professions threw him into bewilderment and self-doubt. He was plagued with feelings of inadequacy, and he questioned his previous success. Having lost the validation of his peers and an ongoing role of importance, his identity had been undermined. It took him nearly a year to come to grips with the questions raised by the job shift. Many people avoid change because they are afraid of losing themselves in the change process.

People who have difficulty handling change in their lives are prone to disappointment. Many of the skills needed to manage disappointment are required for change: awareness, flexibility, resourcefulness and resilience. The ability to make personal change hinges initially on a single question: "Does the power to alter my life originate in me?" and by extension can I stop myself from being disappointed? Without the belief that one's destiny is at least partially self-determined, the ballgame is over before it begins. Fatalists who view themselves as just so many autumn leaves blown about by the winds of karma and DNA have neither the motivation nor the faith to take control of their lives. They see all action as futile since the locus of control is outside themselves. And their position is self-fulfilling. The person who declares: "I have a bad temper; it's just the way I am!" has elected to maintain a specific relationship to her anger. This attitude relieves her of the burden of change but undermines her connection with others. In order to manage disappointment, we must believe in the notion that we can have an impact on our situation, that we are the authors of our actions and beliefs. The French philosopher Jean-Paul Sartre defined responsibility as "being the uncontested author of an event or thing."

In the Chinese language, the character used to indicate the word "crisis" has two meanings: danger and opportunity. Every disappointment is a crisis of sorts and each allows us an opportunity for change. We can deny our feelings, pretend all is well, and hurt privately deep inside. We can also exaggerate the impact of our loss, and dwell on it obsessively. Or we can use our disappointment as a learning tool that can help us to change for the better. As to the danger inherent in every disappointment, nothing could be more dangerous than failing to take advantage of the opportunity to change the dysfunctional expectations that lead to chronic disappointment.

Tom's Story

Tom, a vigorous, highly successful thirty-four-year-old director of training at a multi-national company, provides us with an inside look at a crisis of disappointment that became an opportunity. After years of futile attempts to have a child, Tom learned what neither he nor his wife, Barbara, had initially suspected. The results of a lab test showed that he was infertile and would never be able to father children. For a man in top physical condition who had rarely faced adversity, the news was jolting:

"I can't believe it! Here I am in the prime of my life, running marathons with never so much as a cold, and the doctor tells me I can't produce enough sperm to fertilize a single egg. The idea is totally absurd. I can bike all day, chop a cord of wood, and play basketball for hours, but I can't manage what even a couch potato can do. I don't get it. It doesn't compute."

Tom was defiant. He had always *expected* to father a child and raise a family. The knowledge that his goal was impossible angered and then embittered him. For some time, he refused to believe the diagnosis and demanded repeated verification. When he found conclusively that the sperm counts were accurate, he began to feel confused. The idea of being a father was so fundamental to his expectations for his life that when the possibility was removed he wondered what he would replace it with. He questioned his adequacy as a man and began making self derogatory statements.

Months passed, but he still despaired over his great disappointment. His relationship with Barbara deteriorated. He felt guilty around her. From his perspective, he had let her down and could find no adequate way to compensate her. His sexual interest waned, and he began to show signs of depression. He slept poorly and his interest in work declined.

It was at this point that Tom came to see me. He emphasized his wish to be a father and carry on the family tradition. He wanted to produce a child who resembled him, "an image of myself in the next generation," is how he put it. He felt his circumstances to be terribly unfair. Why had this happened to him? He had never shown signs of physical abnormality. Perhaps the medical opinions were in error after all, and it would only be a matter of time before his wife became pregnant.

It was clear that Tom's predicament was a true crisis of disappointment. He expected to father a child. This goal was not biologically possible, however, and he was profoundly disillusioned. Stuck in the resistance and loss stages of the disappointment cycle, Tom's frustration fed on itself. It grew to such great proportions that it provoked identity questions, shaking the foundation of his self-image. As we tried to change this downward spiral of events, Tom and I had the following conversation:

Tom: *I've been feeling very bad lately. This infertility business has worn me down and confused me. I don't know where I'm going or what I want. I never feel happy. In fact, I rarely feel anything at all. I used to have so much energy. Now I really don't care. It's hard to sort it all out. What's happening to me? I'm worried.*

DB: *When did all this start?*

Tom: *Well, I guess it began when I found out the lab test results. I couldn't believe what the doctor told me. I had thought the problem was my wife's, but as it turned out it was me that had the problem. I can't tell you how let down I felt. Nothing like this had ever happened to me before. I always got what I wanted. But not now.*

DB: *You're disappointed you can't produce children?*

Tom: *Yeah, all my life, I've wanted a family. Sometimes I imagine carrying my child around with me in the neighborhood just so my friends would say, "Your kid's the spitting image of you, Tom." I can't imagine having a meaningful life without them. Why earn money if you can't give it to your children? Why struggle if it's not to make their lives easier? Damn it, the kids are the real reason for living. Without them, I just can't see the purpose.*

DB: *You're saying then that you believe your children will give your life meaning. You assume that without them there is no direction or purpose to your life.*

Tom: *Yeah, but they have to be my children. I have to produce them. I know that's not politically correct, but without your own children, you're just baby-sitting! I'm not interested in a family of other*

people's kids. I don't need that at all. I'm not a
daycare center. Why should I be interested if the kids
aren't mine? (Pause.) Awgh, the whole thing's crazy.

DB: *I hear something in your voice. What are you feeling?*

Tom: *Nothing! What's the use in calling attention to it?*
The whole situation's a mess. It doesn't get any better.
It only gets worse. I really feel terrible about myself.
What good is my success at work or my marriage to
Barbara if I can't have children? I'm a failure, a
washout. This is the most important life function
and I'm deficient. What matters most eludes me.
What matters least I have plenty of. It's not fair. And
no one understands. Friends are no help at all. They
say the wrong thing despite their good intentions.
No, this is something I have to face alone, even
without Barbara. I can't talk to her. She feels sorry
for me, and she's angry at me. And why shouldn't she
be? I can't give her what she wants.

DB: *Let me get this clear. Is your expectation to father*
children biologically possible?

Tom: *I thought for a long time that it was, and I tried all*
sorts of remedies, but if I'm honest with myself I
know it isn't.

DB: *So you're disappointed about something that can't be*
attained no matter what you do.

Tom: *I guess that's true. But I can't seem to give it up.*

DB: *I think you're capable of surrendering the expectation.*
What you really mean is that you still choose not to.
You won't.

Tom: *Okay, I agree. I won't. It's hard to.*

DB: *I know it's hard. You see your expectation of*
fatherhood as essential to you. I wonder if it really is?

Tom: *Of course it is. Nothing's more important to me.*

DB: *There's no question that you want very much to father children and that you seek meaning in your life through fatherhood. But I doubt that either of these wishes is indispensable to your happiness. You would have preferred them, naturally, but they aren't indispensable. I wonder, in fact, how these expectations have limited your experience.*

Tom: *What are you getting at?*

DB: *Well, in placing so much emphasis on family and the fathering of your own children, you seem to have excluded other possibilities from your life which would also provide meaning and significance. For example, creative endeavors, spiritual pursuits, and community service can all give you intrinsic satisfaction and purpose. Fatherhood may be important, but surely it's not everything.*

Tom: *I'm still not convinced. Why shouldn't I get what I want? It's not fair that I shouldn't! Everybody's having unwanted pregnancies, and here Barbara and I want a baby so badly.*

DB: *You give the impression you are entitled to your expectation. That it's something owed to you simply because you strongly desire it.*

Tom: *In a way that's true. I admit it.*

DB: *What do you suppose is the payoff in being disappointed?*

Tom: *Payoff? You must be joking. Why would I want to feel disappointed?*

DB: *It does sound strange, I admit, but it's equally strange that you would hold onto an expectation that's clearly impossible to meet. There must be another reason for doing so — a payoff that we can't easily see.*

Tom: *Yeah, but I can't imagine what it could be.*

DB: *What's the effect of your feeling disappointed?*

Tom: *Well, I'm miserable. That much is clear. And I feel sorry for myself. I feel wronged and victimized, like the world has treated me shabbily.*

DB: *Is there any payoff in that?*

Tom: *Maybe. I feel a bit like a romantic but tragic hero. I have to admit I like those feelings once in a while. Here I am walking around the world seemingly in control of my destiny, but I have one tragic flaw, like Hamlet. It's a strange role. I'm fascinated by it, I guess, but I hardly think it explains why I became disappointed.*

DB: *You're right in the sense that the tragic role may not have motivated you to be disappointed. But once you were, the role became a convenient and attractive way to tolerate your dilemma. Now it's hard to give it up.*

Tom: *I see what you mean. That seems to fit. (Pause)*

DB: *You look deep in thought. What sorts of things are you saying to yourself?*

Tom: *So you think I talk to myself. I'm not that bad off yet!*

DB: *Everyone talks to themselves. Most people do it internally. That's why it's called an internal dialogue. We hardly know it's happening. For example, if I fail an exam I might say to myself, "How stupid can I be? I should have studied harder. Now I'm in real trouble." Or I might say, "The test was unfair; the subject was boring. This is no reflection on me." We*

talk to ourselves as we experience things and in so
doing we influence the way we feel. We interpret our
experiences and then react to those interpretations. I
wonder what you've been saying to yourself.

Tom: *I was thinking a few things as we talked.*

DB: *Such as?*

Tom: *Well, first I thought, "He's just trying to trick me to*
give up what I want. Since there's no orange juice
left, he wants me to be satisfied with apple juice."
That sort of thing. But I still want orange juice. Then
I thought, "I'm not suited for anything but father-
hood. I'm not creative; I don't have any spiritual
leanings. Community service isn't for me. Father-
hood — that's the only thing I can do. If I just had
the chance." After this I began to feel again how
unfair the situation was. I thought to myself, "It's just
not right. I would make such a good father, while
others with children go around abusing them or
taking them for granted."

DB: *All these internal statements show your resistance to*
accepting your situation and making change. You
focus on what you lose rather than what you gain.
You downplay your interest and aptitude for other
meaningful activity. You continue to convince
yourself that fatherhood is indispensable. And you
replay the unfairness of it all when you know full
well that life is rarely just. These statements can help
to forestall change and keep you disappointed. They
prevent acceptance of your dilemma and movement
out of your frustration.

Tom: *I have to accept my situation and give up the impossible expectations. . . well, not so much give them up but change them to something more realistic?*

DB: *That's it.*

Tom: *Well, I've never let myself consider this before, but I can still be a father. Barbara and I could adopt a child or we could use donor sperm. There are other possibilities.*

DB: *That's true. But they only seem viable once you've accepted the failure of your original expectations.*

Tom: *I never saw it that way before.*

DB: *Sometimes for the fog to lift a little wind is necessary.*

Tom: *Now, what does that mean?*

DB: *A Chinese proverb. Think about it.*

Moving Up from Disappointment

Tom eventually accepted his disappointment and created more realistic expectations for himself and the situation. A look back at our conversation will show the steps he took. First, he acknowledged disappointment as the cause of his confusion and turmoil. Then he identified not just the failed expectation but also the deeper wish contained within it. And as he went through these steps, he felt anger and sadness. Eventually he recognized the impossibility of his expectation, but was not yet ready to relinquish it. At this point, I asked a series of questions to help him gain a new perspective on his wishes and to show him how he resisted change by making counterproductive internal statements. Having gone through this process, he was in a position to accept his situation and create a more realistic expectation.

To move up from disappointment, we must follow a similar process:

Acknowledge disappointment

Express feelings

Sort out the issues

Reach acceptance

Move on

Step One: Acknowledge Disappointment

You would think acknowledging disappointment would be a relatively simple process like recognizing an itch or feeling hunger in the pit of your stomach. But as with Willy Loman, the obvious is elusive. Tom knew he was deeply disappointed, but his anger and self-pity were more apparent: They dominated his experience and blocked him from squarely facing his dilemma. It is only by taking the time to ask, "What is at the root of my feeling?" that we can get a glimpse of the sometimes obscure nature of disappointment.

Some people prefer to avoid looking directly at their disappointments. For months Tom held onto the magical belief that his situation would right itself. That action created a series of monthly letdowns as his wife failed to get pregnant. The fact is that facing disappointment is the initial step in moving out of it. Remember that every disappointment is a conflict between wish and reality. The tension that exists between these two contending forces will continue as long as the improbability of the expectation has not been accepted.

Step Two: Express the Emotions

The feelings associated with letdown — anger, hurt, self-pity, loss, dispossession — cannot be denied or suppressed without paying a price, usually the persistence of disappointment. Anyone who has ever tried to avoid bereavement knows that such attempts backfire into depression, confusion, and somatization. Likewise, when couples deny their anger toward each other, their feelings usually result in nitpicking, complaining, or obstinacy. The value of feeling one's emotions is an accepted assumption in our psychologically sophisticated age. Some feelings, however, are hurtful or dangerous. How are these to be expressed without dire consequences? Here are two effective formats, one verbal, one written which help people to express their emotions safely:

Format A: Find a responsible friend who's willing to listen. Select a private spot where sound will not be a problem. Set a time limit and ask your companion to watch the clock for you. Then give yourself permission to express the feelings associated with your disappointment. Don't judge the feelings. Don't try to make them seem reasonable or labor over just the right words. This kind of editing will only get in the way. You have a right to these feelings and your friend has agreed to create a safe haven for their expression. Let them flow without observing yourself. When your friend signals that time is up, inhale very deeply, and relax. Spend ten minutes calming yourself down by breathing deeply to a slow count of six on inhalation, eight on exhalation. If you don't feel some relief, continue the breathing until you experience a sense of lightness. Measure the change in your mood.

If a friend is not available, use the same procedure, imagining that you are talking to such a person.

Format B: Find a private place, free of disturbance. Bring a pen and paper with you. Meditate for a few minutes about your feelings. Visualize yourself at the moment you first experienced the disappointment. Then write about your experience in the present tense, focusing on your emotional reaction. Do you feel anger, frustration, hurt, loss, self-pity, depression? Don't be critical of what you write and don't rework any of it. This is not a short-story contest. The end product is not nearly as important as the process of doing it. Let your feelings flow from your pen.

When you have nothing more to say, sit quietly for a few minutes and measure the effect of the exercise. If you still feel agitated, write about it. If you are more relaxed, move onto the next step in the sequence.

Step Three: Sort Out the Issues

This step has four parts: identifying the expectation, uncovering the lifewish, recognizing the faulty premise, and gaining perspective on the experience.

Identifying the Expectation: Once we have allowed expression of feeling, we must look for the unmet expectation that causes our deepest frustration. Ask yourself, "What am I disappointed about?" "What did I expect to happen?" If nothing is forthcoming, perhaps you don't want to acknowledge the answer. Some expectations are troubling in themselves and can be blocked unconsciously from awareness like the middle-aged bride who expects her groom to be acceptable to her parents but feels guilty or ashamed of such adolescent wishes. Or the lover who expects every sexual experience to be like fireworks on the fourth of July but knows in her bones that such a prospect represents an impossible wish. She may keep herself in the dark as a way to keep her sexual fantasies intact.

Uncovering the Lifewish: Recognizing one's expectations is a relatively straightforward task when compared with exposing the deeper wishes about life that most expectations contain. These desires are artifacts from childhood when we held an innocent view of the world. It is the deeper lifewish within most expectations that hooks us and maintains our emotional investment. Awareness of these wishes is sometimes enough to motivate us to let go of them, but generally we need additional coaxing before we are ready to give them up.

In identifying the wish component within an expectation, we find that a single thought may contain many levels of desire. "I expect my spouse and my parents to get along famously," indicates an obvious desire for the significant people in one's life to like each other. At another level it might represent a wish for interpersonal harmony or a world in which human relations exist without conflict.

Lifewishes have an illusionary character. They are the stuff of fairy tales and dreams that can't come true. Yet I am always surprised at how enduring and resilient they are despite life's harsh treatment of the dreamer. People hold onto irrational wishes as if their lives depended on it. Here are some of the most typical lifewishes. Please feel free to add your own to the list.

The wish:

for life to be easy
for everything to remain the same
for love alone to suffice
for life to be fair
for life to be exciting
for life to be easy
for security
to be saved
to be taken care of
to be special
to be perfect
to be loved by everyone
to live forever
to change the unchangeable
for life to be conflict-free
for things to be as you want them

Recognizing the Faulty Premise: If we did not take lifewishes seriously, did not convert them into operational premises that influence attitude and action, we would not be disappointed by their failure. But these unrealistic yearnings have a way of gaining the upper hand. They easily overrun the slim boundary between what we want and what we expect. For example, the wish for life to be easy, so prominent in the midlife years, is transformed into the illusional belief that life *should, can,* or *will* be easy. Likewise, the desire to be perfect becomes "I can exist without fault." At the root of every disappointment is a lifewish that has been changed into a working-but-faulty premise that fails and causes letdown.

Gaining Perspective: When we are in the throes of disappointment, it is hard to sort out the meaning of the experience. We may exaggerate its importance and endow our disappointments with symbolic implications. A filmmaker patient of mine whose work was inadvertently left out of a press screening feared that his situation was a replay of a hard luck childhood pattern. The thought that he might be falling back into an old and detested *life script* made it hard for him to see his circumstances rationally. By exaggerating the meaning of his lost wish he made it impossible to move on with his life.

It is important to keep your disappointments in perspective. This can be accomplished by taking the following measures:

1. *Viewing each disappointment as a singular event without attaching it to past or future implications.* When disappointment is viewed in this straightforward manner, it does not carry the burden of historical significance or deeper meanings. Having a poem rejected by *The New Yorker* does not mean you'll never be a poet.

2. *Understanding that our expectations are not indispensable to our future happiness.* Of course we prefer that they succeed, but desire and necessity should not be confused. We require food to survive but not a Rolls Royce to transport it home. Tom initially confused the

two, but eventually saw that his life could have meaning without siring children.

3. Recognizing that we are not guaranteed or entitled to our expectations. Just because we expect a good sexual relationship or a high-paying job does not mean we are owed either. To believe we have a right to every wish is to distort our relationship to satisfaction. It is well to remember that we are guaranteed the pursuit of happiness, but not the happiness itself.

Below are three short-order exercises that may be used to gain a new perspective on disappointment.

Observing: Find a comfortable, quiet place and relax for ten minutes, breathing fully and regularly. Close your eyes and image a ball bouncing down a hill. Follow it in your mind's eye. Repeat the sequence several times. Now get an image of a pen slowly writing your name. Follow the motion of the pen. Repeat several times.

Consider this thought: Each of us is a composite of many sub-selves which taken together compose our personality. There is the innocent child, the seeker, the courageous hero, the rescuer, and so forth. Become aware of the disappointed part of yourself, the resigned, crestfallen side of you. Allow an image of this self to emerge. Don't push to create the image or judge it. Just observe this self as if you were watching it on a television screen. What does it look like? What are the feelings that emanate from it? Allow it to speak to you and listen carefully to its response and tone of voice. Now let the image fade away into the background. Be aware of what you feel.

Loosely based on the psychosynthesis techniques of Roberto Assagioli, this exercise requires you to observe the disappointed part of yourself as if it were separate from you. Assagioli's idea is that the act of looking demands disassociation from what you're looking at. Once the disappointed self is split off, it may be observed with dispassion and weakened in much the same way that a fear acknowledged becomes less powerful.

Reviewing: Find a comfortable, quiet place and relax for ten minutes, breathing fully and regularly. On a piece of paper, write down five past disappointments, each occurring at least one year ago. Write in detail how you felt while these experiences were happening. Consider how you feel about these disappointments today. What does this comparison tell you?

Examining past letdowns helps you become aware of the temporal nature of disappointment and recognize your ability to move beyond a particular loss.

Advising: Find a comfortable, quiet place and relax for ten minutes, breathing freely and regularly. Imagine a detailed scenario in which one of your friends experiences a major disappointment. How does the person react? What feelings does he/she express? Now imagine that he/she approaches you for advice on how to deal with the situation. What would you say? How would you say it so that it could be heard with a receptive ear? Now apply the advice to yourself.

By separating from the personal experience and observing it in the life of another person, you gain a more objective frame of reference. This distance allows the full use of your problem-solving abilities which are harder to access when the disappointment is your own.

Step Four: Reaching Acceptance

The final stage in the disappointment process involves accepting the lost expectation. This does not mean you are necessarily happy with the circumstances or that you tacitly approve of them. It simply means that you accept rather than deny what exists. Only by accepting disappointments can you prevent them from happening again. Tom, for example, could only move on with his life after he had acknowledged the loss of his wishes.

When there is hidden gain in remaining disappointed, resolution may be obstructed. The trouble with "secondary" payoffs is that they are not worth the price of continued disillusionment and resignation. Take, for example, the rejected suitor who holds onto his hurt feelings in order to support a neurotic view of himself as undesirable. Or perhaps he is really playing the role of martyr — someone who has been terribly wronged and enjoys the sense of righteousness that unjust treatment provides. Tom recognized the payoff in his suffering. Despite his complaints, the role of "successful but tragically flawed man" held some attraction for him. In the end, however, he discovered his heartbreaking illusions were unsatisfying and worth relinquishing.

Payoffs come in many shapes and sizes. When we hold onto dashed expectations, we support feelings that are not in our long-range or true interests. Remaining disappointed comes not just from a resistance to accepting the failed outcome but also from the neurotic profit gained by feeling miserable. Individuals who have a need to suffer or wish others to feel sorry for them will be drawn to the odd advantages of getting stuck in disappointment.

Moving On: Rachel's Story

Paradoxically, accepting disappointment is the step that allows us to move on to the creation of second-order expectations. To understand how surrendering failed expectations can help us to gain what we want, let us consider the situation of Rachel, a talented, twenty-seven-year-old actress, who, until she began dating Bob, had never been in a successful long-term relationship. Although they seemed well matched, Bob, divorced just six months before, was hesitant to make a commitment of any sort. He expressed this sentiment almost from the outset. Rachel accepted the situation but did not really appreciate the depth of his feelings. She continued to hope that with time he would warm to the idea of a deeper involvement. She assumed the divorce had left temporary wounds that eventually would heal.

The couple usually spent two evenings a week together and frequently called each other on off-days. They shared an interest in the performing arts, often went to museums and galleries, and spent long hours discussing politics. They agreed on almost everything but the current state of their relationship, a subject they avoided by unspoken mutual consent. When Bob suggested they travel together across the country on a shared vacation, Rachel jumped at the chance. She saw it as a real opportunity to deepen their ties and cement their commitment to each other. With enthusiasm, she set about planning every detail of the trip. She investigated the most scenic routes, made all the necessary reservations, and planned amusing day-excursions. Excited by the odyssey, she looked forward to the trip with anticipation. So much relaxed, quality time together, she thought, would be good for the relationship.

But as the departure date approached, Bob became less available. He blamed his inaccessibility on the pressures of finishing a specific work project before the vacation. Rachel was disappointed but accepted the explanation. When they finally drove over the bridge and out of town, she assumed he would relax and reconnect. Indeed, the deepening of their intimacy was her primary wish for the vacation. She was hoping for more than just a good time.

But it didn't happen that way. Although they sat only two feet apart in the car, Bob seemed cooler and more distant than she could ever remember. At the Grand Canyon she attempted to confront his withdrawal, but he changed the subject and she gave up without trying again. A pattern emerged. They were both cheerful in the morning, but fatigued and mildly depressed by afternoon. They carried on conversations about the usual subjects, the natural wonders they were seeing and the variegated sea of tourists around them, but the moment Rachel broached the issue of their relationship, Bob withdrew and became moody. After a while, she simply resigned herself to superficial conversation. When they returned home, she withdrew to her apartment, took a long walk, and found herself crying.

Rachel recognized her disappointment and the expectation that had gone unmet. In spite of her awareness of Bob's ambivalence toward their relationship, she had hoped he would come around as they spent more time together. As things turned out, it was an unrealistic hope, but Rachel refused to be daunted by her disappointment. She cried and felt the pain of her lost wishes, but she determined not to stay caught up in her misery.

She evaluated her situation and saw that although her expectations for the trip had failed, her desire for a more committed relationship was still attainable if she took different action. Of course, if she simply went on as usual, nothing would change. For all she knew, Bob might behave in the same manner indefinitely. No, if she really wanted a deeper commitment, she would have to deal differently with the situation.

Rachel weighed the price of pursuing a more serious relationship with Bob and decided it was worth the risk in possible rejection and greater disappointment. Her plan was to talk to him about what had happened in a relaxed, no-blame atmosphere where they both could express their feelings openly. She called him and arranged for a long dinner at her place. All afternoon she was anxious, but after he arrived she summoned her courage and revealed her disappointment. Bob responded to her candor with forthrightness; he was feeling guilty and needed to clear his own conscience. He confessed that although the vacation initially sounded like a good idea, as time approached he became more nervous about it. He felt trapped by the thought of spending long hours together in the car. He imagined that his resolve to move slowly would be worn down by all the time together and he would be forced to make a commitment he wasn't ready for. As a result, he kept his distance by withdrawing emotionally. He knew she was upset by his actions, but he feared the possibility of unwanted commitment even more.

As they talked openly, both recognized that a genuine affection existed between them. Speaking honestly and from the heart had cleared the air. Rachel understood for the first time Bob's fears and anxieties left over from the divorce. Bob realized that if he showed his vulnerability, Rachel would not overwhelm or manipulate the situation for her own gain. The talk placed the relationship on a new level, and the emotional bond between the two was strengthened without Rachel pushing or Bob feeling threatened. A positive experience was born out of disappointment.

Looking Back

Because disappointment is a particular form of loss, moving through it — from acknowledgement to acceptance — follows a specific pattern. It is only after we accept the loss of our wishes that we are free enough to create new, educated expectations in order to prevent recurrences of disappointment. For people like Tom who refuse to relinquish their expectations even while recognizing their impossibility, the four-step process is a good road map. Using it, they can express their feelings, "reframe" their expectations and move on. Ultimately, accepting disappointment requires surrendering the belief that all one's desires require satisfaction. Once we have abandoned this deeply held wish, we are better able to accept not only our immediate disappointment but the nature of life as well.

Chapter 11

Making Disappointment Work for You

Failure is, in a sense, the highway to success, inasmuch as every discovery of what is false leads us to seek earnestly after what is true, and every fresh experience points out some form of error which we shall afterward carefully avoid.

— John Keats

Most people view disappointment as a negative, irredeemable experience without value or merit. Like mildew, a sprained ankle, or a broken seat at the movie theater, they consider it a regrettable condition to be avoided whenever possible. In chronic form, disappointment is more than regrettable. It is a bridge that links resignation with despair, a causeway to melancholia and depression. Yet, in its milder versions, disappointment does have a positive side. More than that, it is quite functional and plays a very important role in all human endeavor. Disappointment can actually be an ally in the search for contentment and personal happiness. Provided we use it to our advantage and don't allow it to take on chronic proportions, it has value as a teacher and motivator. Disappointment can work for you. Those who have learned from it in the past have less of it in their future. They seem to move through it more rapidly.

The Value of Negative Experience

Most experience, whether positive or negative, has something to teach us. Bad experiences usually convey a more urgent message because they are threatening, frustrating, or anxiety-provoking. As behavioral psychologists point out, how we respond in the present is determined to a large extent by the learning (or conditioning) in our past. Suppose you burn your tongue while eating a steaming bowl of soup. Next time you'll probably wait until the soup cools or, at least, blow on the spoon to cool down its contents. Negative experience has warned you of the consequences of a particular action. It has provided a lesson about soup and perhaps about impatience. Because of your burnt tongue, you are a wiser, albeit more cautious, diner. Bad experience also shakes you out of lethargy. Human beings tend to be creatures of habit. Sometimes we move through life in a walking sleep, repeating the same actions week in and out, and even using the same body motions to do so. The human capacity for repetition is enormous. Most of us repeat, with only minor variations, a workday sequence from the sound of the alarm clock to the moment of sleep sixteen or so hours later. Our existence is ritualized in this manner to avoid discomfort and anxiety, but often we risk becoming mechanized, complacent, and dull, trading excitement for security. A negative experience is like a slap in the face or a drenching in ice water. It wakes us up to our surroundings again, calls forth our energy, and challenges us to new action. The benefits of this reawakening sometimes outweigh the consequences of the bad experience.

In the process of reacting, we must reassess our situation. This evaluation can produce healthy change. We stop taking our lives for granted and begin to act with intention and awareness. For example, when someone we love dies, we feel prolonged, deep grief. But the process of loss provides some benefit as well. It readjusts our priorities and clarifies what is important. Trivial concerns and worries fade away. They seem inconsequential by comparison with the loss of life. Death offers survivors a message about how to proceed with the business of living. It tells them that life is too short and precarious to spend on useless and mundane struggles.

Similarly, frustration — another negative condition we try to avoid — is invaluable in aiding psychological growth, especially during infancy and early childhood. Psychiatrist Margaret Mahler has suggested that frustration, balanced with a positive relationship to the mother, helps to develop the child's autonomy and ego strength. It fosters the infant's maturity by nudging her on to new action independent of the help of her primary parent. Such a level of frustration must be strong enough to develop conflict solving capacities by forcing the child to seek her own solutions, and weak enough to allow the new baby some gratification and comfort. In adulthood, the situation is basically similar. Some frustration sharpens our intellect and discourages indolence. Too much is overwhelming and undermines us.

Heinz Kohut shared a similar point of view. He theorized that the healthy development of self is fostered by what he called "optimal frustrations" — failures in achieving what one desires. These disappointments are precisely what the child requires to grow a robust, competent sense of self that can face the rigors of adult life. Kohut believed that identical optimal frustrations reoccur during psychotherapy and provide — if handled properly by the therapist — another opportunity for the self to be strengthened.

Disappointment, as a negative experience, shakes us up and provokes reassessment of our circumstances. But it does much more than this: It functions in our behalf by teaching us about the limits of possibility, motivating us to take positive action, and strengthening our sense of self.

Our First Teacher

How do we learn about the limits of reality? Psychologists differ considerably on this issue, but folk knowledge is quite clear. Life itself teaches us, with a bit of help from teachers and formal education. Consider how this process occurs. During the first months of life, the infant's bodily sensations are all that is real to it. Hunger, pain, fatigue, delight are the infant's entire universe. Even the primary parent is experienced as part of self. Slowly and inconsistently, the infant begins to distinguish objects. As this gradual process takes place, the baby's developing sense of reality outside itself is actually encouraged by disappointment. In fact, Freud, in his paper "Formulations in the Two Principles of Mental Functioning" (1911), writes that it is disappointment over not getting expected satisfaction that leads the child to supplement fantasy with objective evaluation and judgement of the external world — the "reality principle." Put simply, early disappointment motivates the infant to investigate and evaluate the world. By using memory, perception, and thought, it learns to distinguish what is real from what is imagined. Over time, the child becomes proficient at sizing up reality.

Disappointment also educates us about the reality of possibility. It is through the process of losing an expectation that we learn what is possible. As a young boy, I once sent in a cereal boxtop to get a genuine Canadian Mountie badge. The next day I went to the mailbox to search for my gift. It wasn't there. I was stricken with disappointment. I complained for hours. It ruined my day and, needless to say, my mother's. By the time the badge arrived six weeks later, I had learned a powerful and important lesson. Expectations of immediate gratification are not always met. Sometimes we simply have to wait. Not only did I develop an understanding of delayed reward (and incidentally, the vagaries of postal service), but I also began to see that merely expecting (wishing) did not produce a result.

We might think of disappointment as a "possibility meter." Each loss of expectation gives us a reading on how well we have assessed possibility. If an expectation fails, it tells us something about its attainability. Paying attention to this feedback, we can learn to avoid disappointment in the future by shaping our expectations differently. We may find that X is attainable and Y is possible only under certain circumstances, or we may realize that none of our expectations is realistic. We need only read the meter.

A friend of mine, Sarah, used an experience of disappointment to create new, more realistic expectations. Her lover of two months failed to show up for an exhibition of her paintings. This was an important event in her life, and she was disappointed and resentful. She accepted his inadequate excuse, though she trusted him less because it seemed like a false alibi. At another showing of her work three months later, he was again conspicuously absent. Sarah was let down once more, but this time she opened her eyes to the lesson contained in her disappointment. She recognized that her expectations for an intimate and sharing relationship with this man were probably unrealistic. She wanted a partner who would be more interested in her life and take her involvement in art seriously. She was faced with a choice: change the expectation or exchange the man. Her disappointment meter had told her twice that he was not reliable or interested in an important part of her identity.

Disappointment is the sort of condition we would prefer to avoid. Yet experiencing it gives us the opportunity to fine tune our view of possibility. Ironically, those who learn from dashed expectations are those who avoid chronic disappointment. The best teacher of how to avoid disappointment is disappointment itself.

Consider the educational value of disappointment in another way — as a cold shower that dampens our illusions and wishes. Our childhood hopes are carried around like old baggage on life's journey, and we are hard-pressed to give them up. They color every expectation. We have already encountered many of them: the wish for life to be fair, people to remain the same, love alone to sustain us. Disappointment teaches us that these wishes have no basis in reality and that we need to surrender our view that their fulfillment is, in fact, possible.

By putting the damper on our expectations, disappointment forces us to reevaluate our wants. This process encourages maturity. Illusions hold us back from embracing life as it is. The thirty-two-year-old man who is disappointed in how quickly he is aging looks in the mirror each morning and sees wrinkles on his forehead and crow's feet around his eyes. Why is he disappointed? He had expected to appear youthful through middle age. At the root of the expectation may be a wish for prolonged youth — to hold back the hands of time. The quest for immortality, the most vain of all human desires, plagues our youth-oriented culture, especially as baby boomers move into their fifties. Witness the phenomenal growth of anti-aging remedies, herbs and extracts, tinctures and eye tucks. In our society, the ideal standard of female beauty is too young to vote. Youth is equated with desirability and value. No wonder the man wishes to remain young. The experience of observable aging disturbs him. His deeper wish cannot be satisfied. Only if he is receptive to the lesson contained in his disappointment will he realize that the deeply etched lines on his face will not disappear. His wish for eternal youth is illusory and must be relinquished to avoid greater frustration. His disappointment provides him with an invitation to reevaluate his unrealistic expectations.

The central illusion at the root of all disappointment is the belief that as individuals we have the right to have all our needs and desires fulfilled. Failed expectation is a form of non-gratification, a narcissistic injury. We do not get what we think we deserve. Yet, in reality, we cannot always have what we want. Sometimes we must wait for satisfaction. Other times even waiting will not produce the desired result. All disappointment defies the illusional wish that we are entitled to a particular outcome. Disappointment says to us that we are not special, but human like everyone else and subject to the laws of nature. There are limits to gratification. Perhaps this is disappointment's most important lesson.

There is yet another way in which disappointment can be useful, a way which offers an independent study course in self. By analyzing your disappointments you learn a great deal about your own character. (See Chapters 6, 7, and 8 for more on this.) Chronic patterns of disappointment are as revealing as responses to a Rorschach ink blot. They tell us what we expect from life and from ourselves. Repeated disappointment in not receiving enough recognition, for example, may indicate an underlying wish to be special or a deep need to gain the constant approval of others. Recurrent disappointment in oneself suggests a lack of confidence and a self-critical nature. The clues are observable. Try this exercise yourself.

Self Study

1. Write down the three most significant disappointments in your life.
2. Identify the unmet expectations.
3. Identify any deeper wishes at the root of each expectation.

4. Look for patterns in your expectations. What do these
   expectations reveal about you?
5. How attainabe are your expectations? Is there a   pattern
in the degree of attainability? If so, what does it   indicate about
your grasp of realistic possibility? What
          else does the pattern suggest about you?
6. What actions would bring your expectations to fruition?
   Since you haven't taken such action, what does this reveal
   about you? Learning about ourselves from disappointment proceeds along three lines:

   ▪ the pattern of desire in our expectations.

   ▪ the degree of realism in our expectations.

   ▪ the degree of passivity that we show in not
     acting to satisfy our desires.

   Our style of disappointment provides us with important
information about ourselves. The problem is we don't always pay
attention. We resent our disappointments, complain about them,
and let them control us. We don't see them as useful tools to help
us avoid future pain. When we simply try to forget them as rapidly
as possible, we fail to learn from them. We might paraphrase the
popular words of George Santayana to read, "Those who cannot
learn from disappointment are condemned to repeat it."

Disappointment as Motivator

   Although some people seem to literally stew in disappointment's unsavory juices, others are inspired by their
discomfort to take action. Feminist Lucy Stone describes how
disappointment was a galvanizing force in her life:

   *From the first years to which my memory stretches, I have
   been a disappointed woman. When, with my brothers, I*

reached forth after sources of knowledge, I was reproved with, "It isn't fit for you; it doesn't belong to women." In education, in marriage, in religion, in everything, disappointment is the lot of women. It shall be the business of my life to deepen this disappointment in every woman's heart until she bows down to it no longer.

Stone's disappointment had a paradoxical effect. Frustration, anger, and pain ignited in her a passion for change. Her emotional losses became so intolerable that she was galvanized to action. Like homeopathic remedies which cure by prescribing more of the symptom, her experience will not produce the same result in everyone. Paradoxical interventions work best when the individual is strong enough to tolerate repeated frustrations, or when there is powerful resistance to change and everything else has failed. Given the choice most people would avoid an increase in disappointment even to achieve the longer-range goal of well-being.

Disappointment has the capacity to improve problem-solving skills. There is the classic example — taught in every Psych 101 class — of the frustrated monkey who sits in his cage while a banana hangs temptingly outside his reach. Try as he may, he can't quite get at it by sticking his arm through the bars. After many disappointments, he notices a stick in the cage. He grabs it, extends it toward the banana, and manipulates it into range. No one has taught him this behavior. Hunger and disappointment combine to motivate the problem-solving sequence. The monkey acts to satisfy his expectation and his appetite. Human beings with greater powers of reasoning are better equipped to attain gratification than their primate cousins. As long as one's expectation is somewhat attainable, the number of problem-solving strategies is endless.

Enhancing Functioning

Adversity strengthens us! Is this old folk wisdom merely a rationalization to help us deal with suffering, or is there psychological truth in it? The answer is qualified. Disappointment may strengthen us. However, a great deal depends on when and how much we are disappointed. During periods of stress and personal vulnerability, added disappointment can overwhelm us. It may take months just to get out from under it. If a person has limited ego resources — low self-esteem or feelings of inadequacy — disappointment is unlikely to fortify him. It will keep him defeated and resigned. Chronic disappointment patterns have much the same effect. They weaken resolve and result in despair. But the single disappointment, experienced by a relatively healthy individual who moves through it, does work to enhance functioning in two ways: It helps him learn how to deal with loss, and it shows him firsthand that he can survive adversity.

As I noted earlier, disappointment involves loss, but not the severe loss of an object, friend, or life. Disappointment is the loss of an idea, an expectation. Without disastrous consequences, it provides the psychological experience of mild bereavement. Disappointment is a safe practice field where we learn to deal with emotional pain without playing for high stakes. It is a valuable rehearsal for managing more significant loss.

Our reaction to adversity functions as a mirror. Within it, we can see our frailty and strength. Those who rise to overcome obstacles are rewarded with a reflection of their own mastery and perseverance. Like athletes who have run their first marathon, they have learned they have what it takes to make it. In the words of Wendell Phillips, "What is defeat? Nothing but education; nothing but the first step to something better." If we take this attitude, we will be strengthened by our struggle.

Another Paradoxical Perspective

Until recently, the Western world has shown little interest in Oriental thought or religion. But as the revolution in tele-communications shrinks the planet and our connection to Asia is strengthened by economic and political bridges, the wisdom of the East has begun to flow into our culture. And nowhere is the experience of disappointment seen as positively as through the eyes of the Buddha.

Buddhism offers a unique perspective on disappointment which is helpful simply by its unusual nature. According to its teachings, life is filled with suffering. Sorrow, grief, dis-satisfaction, decay, disappointment — these are all described in one word — *duhka*. The cause of this pain rests in the way we live our lives. Because we feel something is lacking or incomplete, we are always trying to set it right. We busy ourselves striving to improve our existence, getting more pleasure, and holding on to it to fill this void. We attempt to wipe out duhka by grasping for more and clinging to what we already have. The frenetic desire for pleasure indicated by our emphasis on leisure-time activity and sexuality, the insatiable quest for new adult toys and games, the constant effort toward improving the quality of our lives by expansion and acquisition, these are all signs of grasping for gratification. From the Buddhist point of view, this is an empty struggle. The things that we desire offer us no real satisfaction. They are simply diversions of tinsel and neon devoid of any inherent value. We are continually disappointed because acquiring the new car or the ski condo does not in the long run make us feel better about life. The immediate stimulation they provide wears off quickly and we look again for new gratification. Like the heroin addict, we are on a nerve-racking elevator ride: excitement followed by emptiness. The real problem is our striving.

How to exit this trap? Strangely enough, the answer rests in disappointment itself. Buddhism asserts that the only way we will ever elect to give up our endless pattern of purposeless endeavor is by being utterly disappointed. In this paradoxical approach, only prolonged emotional pain has the power to show us the error of our ways. When we are truly disappointed, drenched in our own frustration, we will then have the motivation to give up our counterproductive lifestyle and move to a more spiritual path. Chogyam Trungpa, a revered Tibetan Buddhist who founded numerous communities in this country, says:

> We must surrender our hopes and expectations as well as our fears, and march directly into disappointment, work with disappointment, go into it and make it our way of life, which is a very hard thing to do. Disappointment is a good sign of basic intelligence. It cannot be compared to anything else: it is so sharp, precise, obvious and direct. If we can open, then we suddenly begin to see that our expectations are irrelevant compared with the reality of the situation we are facing.

Disappointment exhausts us. It wears us down so that finally we relinquish our striving expectations and simply live life without anticipation or plan. We accept life as it is, minute by minute, and give up trying to control it through anticipation or wishes. When we stop clutching at clouds, we put an end to our own frustration.

Of course, there is a deeper level to this road to liberation. In the Buddhist way of thinking, striving to maintain control over our future and seeking continual gratification are secondary issues. The sense of self that we are trying to please is actually a transitory and discontinuous event which we take to be real and solid like an "illusory circle of fire made by a whirling torch." For

Buddhists, the ego does not exist. Disappointment ultimately teaches us this fact by frustrating our attempts to gratify it.

Whether we accept this notion of the impermanent and unknowable self or whether we reject it, Buddhism's message about disappointment provokes us to new ways of thinking about why we are disappointed. Perhaps the continual struggle for more and better gratification is at the root of the problem. As long as we believe the way to personal happiness is through the satiation of every want, we will be trapped in an illusory quest for an impossible satisfaction. Like the phoenix rising from its own ashes, our appetites resurrect themselves after only the briefest of moments. By calling our attention to the self-defeating nature of striving, the Buddhist perspective has value.

Disappointment as Benefactor

Disappointment, the main cause of much frustration and unhappiness, is also a benefactor. It helps us to develop a clearer understanding of the limits of possibility. It shakes us out of our complacency and challenges us to bring our expectations to fruition or surrender them and proceed to other satisfactions. It enhances our functioning by teaching us to deal with loss and providing confidence to survive future adversity.

The experience of disappointment in small doses is a positive sign. It implies that we have enough trust in the future to expect and to hope. A life without any disappointment means that the person has already given up on tomorrow. Nothing is as bleak as the loss of possibility.

It is what we make of our disappointments that determines our future. If we hide from them, we learn nothing. In a sense, we must embrace our disappointments in order to fathom their meaning. With careful observation, we can discover important things about ourselves and the nature of life that will enrich our existence. The individual with fewest disappointments is the one who has learned from past experience. The road away from disappointment involves the creative use of the problem itself.

In a larger sense, disappointment shakes us out of our narcissistic preoccupation with self. It reminds us that gratification of our wishes is not guaranteed and that we are, after all, only human and subject to the vicissitudes of time and chance. In this era of self-exaltation, that is a fair message to take to heart.

A Gift Not a Given

The question "is that all there is?" requires us to examine our basic notions about life. Whether our daily experience is fundamentally disappointing depends not so much on what we achieve, acquire or create but on our larger attitude about being alive. Do we take life itself for granted? Is life seen as a gift or a given?

Most people, unless they are sick or dying, do not awaken each morning with a sense of thanks for another twenty-four hours of consciousness. We have too much to do, too many demands, responsibilities and routines. Life itself simply unfolds without a conscious decision on our part. But imagine how your experience would be transformed if you were continuously aware that life was a gift, something evanescent and recallable at any moment? What happens to disappointment when we appreciate this most elemental fact of existence?

For life is fleeting and precious. Human beings are more vulnerable than they like to think. Advances in medicine, science and technology provide the illusional assurance that everything's under control and we need not worry about tomorrow. But we all know the real story. Every time a friend is diagnosed with cancer, an acquaintance is injured in an auto accident, a celebrity overdoses, a passerby is hit by a stray bullet, we think: "There but for fortune...."

Gratitude for life puts a new perspective on living. Disappointments are less hurtful when weighed against the gift of existence. Unfortunately, gratitude has a platitudinous ring to it. It gives off the mildewed odor of antiquated morals and bygone values. It sounds like a word flung from pulpits and preached by parents of teenagers. Yet for all these pejorative associations, gratitude may be our best bulwark against disappointment especially in a narcissistic era when everyone feels *entitled* to their dreams and goals.

And not just gratitude for life but gratefulness in general. The capacity to appreciate, to see what one has rather than what one is missing should not be underrated. Disappointment fairly evaporates when one appreciates transitory joys like a warm fire on a damp morning, a sympathetic look in a room of strangers, the crinkled first smile on your baby's face. Or enduring things like music, physical vitality, or a well-tended garden. Thankfulness keeps disappointment at bay and keeps life from getting dull or agonizing.

Our popular culture endlessly titillates, stimulates and touts personal gratification. It preaches the three-fold gospel of success, acquisition and fame. It tells us that these things will make us happy beyond our wildest dreams. But what we really need to be happy is to develop an old-fashioned sensibility: the capacity to appreciate what is given. To the question, "Is that all there is?" the appreciative individual answers, "Yes, and it's more than enough."

References

Allen, Woody. (1980). *Side Effects*. New York: Ballantine.

Assagioli, Roberto. (1971). *Psychosynthesis: A Manual of Principles and Techniques*. New York: The Viking Press

Beckett, Samuel. (1954). *Waiting for Godot*. New York: Grove Press.

Berne, Eric, M.D. (1977). *Games People Play*. New York: Grove Press.

Chodorow, Nancy. (1978). *The Reproduction of Mothering*. Berkeley: University of California Press.

Crowley, Goeffrey with Underwood, Anne. (1998). "Healer of Hearts." *Newsweek*, March 16.

Diagnostic and Statistical Manual of Mental Disorders IV. (1994). American Psychiatric Association.

Dinnerstein, Dorothy. (1976). *The Mermaid and the Minotaur*. New York: Harper & Row.

Ekman, Paul, and Friesen, Wallace V. (1984). *Unmasking the Face*. Palo Alto, California: Consulting Psychologists Press

Ellis, Albert, and Harper, Robert A. (1975). *A New Guide to Rational Living*. Hollywood: Wilshire Book Co.

Erikson, Erik. (1993). *Childhood and Society*. New York: W.W. Norton.

Fagan, Joen, and Shepherd, Irma Lee. (1970). *Gestalt Therapy Now*. New York: Harper & Row.

Feldenkrais, Moshe. (1990). *Awareness Through Movement*. San Francisco: HarperSanFrancisco .

Ferrucci, Piero. (1983). *What We May Be*. New York: Putnam.

Freud, Sigmund. (1961). "Formulation on the Two Principles of Mental Functioning." Standard Edition. London: Hogarth Press.

Freud, Sigmund. (1952). *A General Introduction to Psychoanalysis*. Translated by Joan Riviere. New York: Washington Square Press.

Freud, Sigmund. (1961). *Civilization and Its Discontents*. Translated by James Strachey. New York: W.W. Norton & Co.

Friedan, Betty. (1974). *The Feminine Mystique*. New York: W.W. Norton.

Fromm, Erich. (1956). *The Art of Loving*. New York: Bantam.

Haley, Jay. (1987). *Problem Solving Therapy,* 2nd Edition. San Francisco: Jossey-Bass.

Herrick, Neal. (1981). "How Dissatisfied is the American Worker?" *Society.* January/February.

Hinsie, Leland E., and Campbell, R.J. (1981). *Psychiatric Dictionary.* 5th edition. New York: Oxford University Press.

Holmes, T.H., and Rahe, R.H. (1967). "The Social Readjustment Rating Scale." *Journal of Psychosomatic Research, No. 11.*

Horn, Jack. (1978). "Smaller Is Better." *Psychology Today,* June.

Jones, Landon Y. (1980). *Great Expectations.* New York: Ballantine.

Kazantzakis, Nikos. (1952). *Zorba the Greek.* Translated by Gerald Wildman. New York: Simon and Schuster.

Keen, Sam. (1980). *What to Do When You're Bored and Blue.* New York: Wyden Books.

Kelly, James. (1982). "Unemployment on the Rise." *Time,* February 2.

Kierkegaard, Soren. (1959). *Either/Or.* Translated by David F. Swenson and Lillian Marvin Swenson. Garden City, New York: Doubleday.

Kohut, Heinz. (1978). *The Search for The Self, Volume 1..* Madison, Connecticut: International Universities Press, Volume 1.

Kopp, Sheldon. (1978). *An End to Innocence.* New York: MacMillan.

Kubler-Ross, Elisabeth. (1981). *On Death and Dying.* New York: Macmillan.

Lasch, Christopher. (1979). *The Culture of Narcissism.* New York: Norton.

LoPicolo, Joseph, and LoPicolo, Leslie, editors. (1978). *Handbook of Sex Therapy.* New York: Plenum Press.

Lowen, Alexander. (1994). *Bioenergetics.* New York: Penguin.

Lowen, Alexander. (1971). *The Language of the Body.* New York: Collier.

May, Rollo. (1994). *The Courage to Create.* New York: Norton.

May, Rollo. (1989). *Love and Will.* New York: Doubleday.

McLuhan, Marshall. (1994). *Understanding Media.* New York: MIT Press.

McLuhan, Marshall. (1996). *The Medium Is the Message.* New York: Bantam.

Maloney, Lawrence D. and McCann, John J. (1982). "Middle Age, the Best of Times," *U.S. News and World Report,* October 25.

Miller, Arthur. (1976). *Death of a Salesman.* New York: Penguin.

Morgenthau, Hans, and Persons, E. (1978). "The Roots of Narcissism." *Partisan Review, XLV:3.*

"Newsline." (1982). *Psychology Today,* April.

Ornstein, Robert E., editor. (1973). *The Nature of Human Consciousness*. San Francisco: W.H. Freeman.

"The Other Half. Partners in Pain." (1982). *American Health*, May/June.

Pelletier, Kenneth. (1977). *Mind as Healer, Mind as Slayer*. New York: Delta.

Piaget, Jean. (1974). *The Construction of Reality in the Child*. Translated by Margaret Cook. New York: Ballantine.

Piaget, Jean and Inhelder, Barbel. (1972). *Psychology of the Child*. New York: Basic Books.

"Poll Results: On the job." (1980). *Saturday Review, May*.

Reich, Wilhelm. (1980). *Character Analysis*, Revised Ed. Translated by Vincent R. Carfagno. New York: Farrar, Straus, & Girous.

Reich, Wilhelm. (1980). *The Mass Psychology of Fascism*. Translated by Vincent R. Carfagno. New York: Farrar, Straus, & Giroux.

Reik, Theodor. (1976). *Masochism in Sex and Society*. New York: Pyramid.

Schumer, Fran R. (1982). "Downward Mobility." *New York Magazine*, August.

Shapiro, David. (1972). *Neurotic Styles*. New York: Basic Books.

Sheehy, Gail. (1984). *Passages*. New York: Bantam.

Sheler, Jeffery L. (1981). "Why So Many Workers Lie Down on the Job." *U.S. News and World Report*, April 6.

Trungpa, Chogyam. (1987). *Cutting through Spiritual Materialism*. Boulder and London: Shambhala Publications.

U.S. National Center for Health Statistics. (1998). "Vital Statistics of the United States," Annual.

Watts, Alan. (1957). *The Way of Zen*. New York: Vintage.

Watts, Alan. (1969). *Psychotherapy East and West*. New York: Ballantine.

"Why Some People Can't Love." (1978). Linda Wolfe interview with Otto Kernberg. *Psychology Today, June*.

Yankelovich, Daniel. (1982). *New Rules*. New York: Bantam Books.

Index

MORE BOOKS WITH *IMPACT*

We think you will find these Impact Publishers titles of interest:

Please see the following page for more books.